GENTLE AND FIERCE

Also by Vanessa Berry

Mirror Sydney
Ninety9
Strawberry Hills Forever

VANESSA BERRY

GENTLE AND FIERCE

Published 2021
from the Writing and Society Research Centre
at Western Sydney University
by the Giramondo Publishing Company
PO Box 752
Artarmon NSW 1570 Australia
www.giramondopublishing.com

Illustrations by Vanessa Berry

Designed by Jenny Grigg
Typeset by Andrew Davies
in Tiempos Regular 9/15pt

Printed and bound by Ligare Book Printers
Distributed in Australia by NewSouth Books

A catalogue record for this book is available from the National Library of Australia.

ISBN 978-1-925818-71-0

9 8 7 6 5 4 3 2 1

The Giramondo Publishing Company acknowledges the support of Western Sydney University in the implementation of its book publishing program.

This project has been assisted by the Commonwealth Government through the Australia Council, its arts funding and advisory body.

‘Gentleness is a relationship to time that finds in the very pulsation of the present the feeling of a future and a past reconciled, that is, of a time that is not divided. This reconciled time makes life possible.’

Anne Dufourmantelle, *Power of Gentleness*

Gentle
&
Fierce

Contents

Compound Eye

Compound Eye

The eye that sees through time observes how the past braids into the present and how it shapes what is to come. Like the compound eye of an insect, it perceives all directions at once. Through this eye I see how memories curl and twist around details and moments, observing how they connect up and constellate.

With this way of seeing I notice how animals have shaped my life. In my childhood my animals were the teddy bears that I believed might come to life when I wasn't looking, and the wise badgers or reckless toads of children's books. I chased the silvery garden skinks that ran over rocks, imagining I could be quick enough to catch them. Then, as a teenager, I was drawn to the shadowy and the nocturnal. I wore dresses with black skirts like the wings of the bats that flew over at twilight, and felt an accord with the ravens that perched on the electricity wires, cawing long and low.

In my adult life my animals have been those that, like me, have the city as a home. There are the daily birds, the ibis and magpies and pigeons. There are the insects, the ants that course over the kitchen bench, the mosquitos that come to whine in my ear and keep me awake, and the spiders that startle me as they dart out across the walls of my room. There are the dogs that I have shared walks with, and the black cat that comes up to me whenever I sit in the garden, appearing in a blink, as if she has materialised from out of nowhere.

Through paying attention to animals and their constant presence comes a heightened awareness that we inhabit a shared world. Animals themselves, the objects that are made in their likenesses, and the ways humans describe animals and their lives, all form a part of it. With this comes an awareness of qualities, the descriptions for styles of behaviour which are used in definition of human and animal identities.

Gentleness and ferocity are two qualities which guide my experiences. Gentleness, with its quiet power, is a hidden strength. To be gentle is to resist the privileging of command above compassion. It is a quiet voice, a persistent whisper, calm and consoling. Ferocity is an armour, a forceful expression of resolve and protection. To be fierce is to know the intensity of the edges of feeling. It is the voice that calls out, intending to be heard. Gentleness and ferocity push and pull at each other, working together as life forces.

I recognise how gentleness and ferocity thread through the stories of my life, which are as much the stories of connections with others, human and non-human, as mine alone. Examining my experiences, turning them around and into new configurations, I envisage them radiating out into a web of life. Within this animals are always present, sometimes quiet, sometimes insistent, but always there.

Forces and connections can be observed within the smallest of objects, moments and encounters. By training ourselves to see this, by bringing attention to the details of our lives and giving voice to their extended stories, we can harness our energies, both gentle and fierce, towards care for the living world.

The Butterfly Effect

The Butterfly Effect

If names shape destinies, mine has in part been shaped by butterflies. At first I knew my name as a sound, three syllables finishing in a soft hiss before the stop of the 'a'. I learned to write it, the double 's's curling like caterpillars. When I consulted a book of names and their meanings, and found Vanessa to mean butterfly, this fact was a gift hidden inside my identity.

Before Vanessa came to mean butterfly it began as an endearment created by Jonathan Swift for his lover Esther Vanhomrigh. By switching the first syllables of her two names and running them together he composed a new name that was emblematic of their private world. They wrote passionate letters to each other, and although their romance was fraught with tension and uneven affections, Swift wrote a long poem, *Cadenus and Vanessa,* in their honour. The name Vanessa remained between them alone until after her death, when *Cadenus and Vanessa* was published. After this the name flew free. A century later it caught the attention of a Dutch entomologist who chose it for a genus of butterfly, the colourful species commonly known as admirals and painted ladies. It was in this way that the name Vanessa came to represent butterflies, and to flutter from name, to butterfly, and then to name again.

Sharing a name with an animal, as with any deliberate act of attention to something particular, attunes you to their presence. Vanessas flit past me with light movements of their bright wings and I see myself in them. I think of them in times when I am carried along by circumstances rather than my intentions, and let them guide me. Let go, I tell myself, surrender to the flow of things, like butterflies are carried by the wind, and scent and colour provide their direction.

As a child, to account for the shyness that saw me fit so poorly into social situations, I would console myself with the fact that I was part butterfly. They were my namesakes and with them I could drift. Any mention of butterflies was a story intended for me, and so I'd go searching for them. On the bookshelf in the study were two tall stacks of *National Geographic* magazines. My parents had subscribed to it for decades and there was a complete set from the 1970s, their yellow spines listing the contents in intriguing combinations: Mount St Helens, Ancient Ashfall, Wildlife Refuges, Bulgaria, Giant Otters. It seemed there was no place or topic that wouldn't eventually come to the magazine's encyclopaedic attention. I travelled across the maps of the stars or the ocean floor or into the photographs of cities and forests and people living their daily lives in Kunming or Veracruz. Later, as an adult, I realised the limitations of the magazine's approach, and how many of the articles and photographs showed me ethnographic stereotypes, but as a child I found in them a way to imagine the wider world and its places, people and animals.

The front cover of the August 1976 issue was a photograph of a woman sitting among monarch butterflies clustered on the tree trunks to either side of her. There is such a density of orange wings that she seems to be within a throne of autumn leaves. She gazes down towards her outstretched hands, where monarchs have settled on her upturned fingers. I imagined being her, surrounded by so much tremulous life, and how I would sit perfectly still, like the trunks of the great fir trees around me, for as long as it took for the butterflies to cover me completely.

The photograph had been taken in an area of forest deep in the mountains of Central Mexico, where the butterflies spend the winter after their migration from North America. At the centre of the photograph, amid the masses of butterflies, was Catalina Aguado, the woman who had found this secluded and elusive place. The article's author, the Canadian zoologist Fred A. Urquhart, had enlisted Aguado to help him find the monarchs' overwintering place. For decades Urquhart and his wife Norah had coordinated the tagging of the butterflies, sending out tiny adhesive labels to volunteers to attach to monarchs' wings, in an attempt to track their migration. Then for two years Aguado and her husband followed the trail of the monarchs into a remote part of the mountains in Michoacán, until they came upon the place where millions of butterflies carpeted the trees and the ground like snow.

When I look around in second-hand bookstores and op shops I find past issues of *National Geographic* in plentiful supply. Although outdated, their lavish photographs and thick, glossy pages give them endurance, as volumes worth keeping rather than discarding. Their yellow spines still promise categorical knowledge of the world, and often among them I find this issue that shows Catalina Aguado surrounded by butterflies, looking down, concentrating on her hands stretched out in front of her and the monarchs that have alighted on them. Coming upon this image again, I see it as a record of past abundance. Magazine articles about monarchs now either promote the tourist experience of the overwintering sites, or the butterflies' decline amid the insect apocalypse wrought by climate change.

Back at the bookshelf at home, along with the *National Geographics*, I found *Gulliver's Travels* by Jonathan Swift. I was too young to understand it as a satire and read it as if it were a history, rather than a fantasy. My favourite section was Gulliver's journey to Brobdingnag, in which he finds himself proportionally tiny beside the immense humans and animals of a giant world. As well as the sixty-foot-high humans of Brobdingnag there were rats as large as dogs and flies the size of birds. Animals which he could once easily control or avoid were now immense and menacing. To protect Gulliver the queen of Brobdingnag has a cabinet maker construct a miniature wooden box as his living quarters. When a cloud of wasps is attracted by the crumb of cake that he is eating at the box's open window, Gulliver draws his sword and fights off these massive insects, fearing for his life.

Being at the age when dolls' houses and miniature porcelain ornaments were of fascination to me, I often imagined what life would be like if I existed on that tiny scale. It was easy enough to locate objects with which I could furnish my surroundings. I could use a cotton reel for a table, a matchbox for a bed, a shoebox for a house. I could travel in the shirt-front pockets of obliging friends, peering out through the fibres of the fabric, secretly watching all that occurred in the regular world.

Some features of the suburban landscape hinted at the co-existence of Brobdingnag. Decorating the front wall of a neighbour's house was a trio of large ornamental butterflies, each half a metre across. They were shaped out of metal with springs of wire for antennae, their wings painted in the brown and black leadlight pattern of monarchs. They rested on a wooden cottage which looked little changed from the 1950s. The house was painted pale pink and fenced by a low, wrought-iron railing shaped into a pattern of hearts and curls. Going past it I'd stare at the butterflies, willing their wings to move, thinking how, when I was an adult, I would live in such a house, under the sign of the butterfly.

Adulthood would be a time of emergence, as if from a cocoon, into a life in which I was colourful and unconstrained. Or so I had hoped. Instead it was not so great a shift. Into my twenties, then thirties, I still felt as ponderous as ever, given to reticence in social situations and to slinking away alone. The houses I lived in were those of the cockroach, the ant, and the pantry moth, all of which were my plentiful co-inhabitants. Their ugly facades faced baldly onto the street, or hid behind the kinds of straggly unloved bushes that sprouted up beside inner-city houses as if they were seeded by them. Inside there were mouldy walls and taps that dripped no matter how often they were attended to. There was a sense of time and energy going sour, seeping away. These houses felt temporary, places to wait for life to start, even when I lived in the same one for years on end.

In the last years of my twenties I lived in a house directly under the western flight path into the nearby airport, over which planes flew so low that the windows shook. In the front garden, visible through the shuddering glass, was the consolation of a hibiscus tree with lavish orange flowers. Butterflies visited it, black-and-white swallowtails with their hindwings patterned with red dots, or sometimes my namesakes would arrive, yellow admirals, *Vanessa itea*, orange and black with one blue spot on each of their wings like all-seeing eyes. They flew with light, loose unconcern even when the planes were howling overhead.

Every object I'd accumulated over my lifetime surrounded me in this one room overlooking the hibiscus tree. The volume of things stacked up in Tetris-like arrangements created an atmosphere of random assortment: a mess, to put it plainly. That most of it had been found second-hand was a comfort, as if its previous ownership had given the objects a wisdom I might unlock and put to use. I was drawn to kitsch, ancillary things, remnants from the 1970s that had decorated suburban homes in the era I was born. Most were trifling objects, ultimately dispensable, along with a few objects that I regarded as truly precious. Among these was a collection of butterflies.

The butterflies were enclosed in a deep wooden frame, sealed under glass. Pinned to a burgundy velvet backboard, they were arranged by size and colour into three rows that curved upwards, suggesting the arc of flight. Each one was suspended by a silver pin speared through its thorax, invisible unless you looked closely, so the butterflies seemed to be floating within the frame. On the back was affixed a page with decoratively burnt edges, giving the paper an artificial patina of age. In tiny handwriting and hair-thin ink each entry on the label listed the name of the butterfly and the place and date it had been captured, and an attribution, 'All butterflies personally caught and mounted by S.P. Lamond'.

Around a third of the butterflies were from a suburban garden in Sydney which I assumed had belonged to the collector. One of these local butterflies was a common imperial blue, with delicate tails curling from its lower wings. It was caught, the description reported, after it hatched from a pupa found on a wall at a train station in December 1970. I could imagine the scene, the collector spying the cocoon attached to the bricks of the station building, detaching it and wrapping it in a handkerchief, slipping it into a bag or a suitcase to take home. Other specimens came from South America. An amber-coloured *Dryas iulia* had been captured while sipping moisture with others of the same species at Caranavi in Bolivia, and a monarch had been caught flying in a cleared field next to the river in Palma Real, Peru. With each description I imagined the swoop of the net and the butterfly transferred to the killing jar with a deft pinch of the collector's practised fingers.

The collection presented life and death intertwined. These butterflies were a diary of sorts, with the experience of their pursuit captured along with each of them. When I moved my eyes across them my thoughts swung between two responses: joy at their beauty, distress at their lifelessness. I couldn't imagine catching and stilling such fragile lives and claiming them as mine.

I was a different kind of collector, my own butterflies being the observations I recorded in my journals. By the time I lived in the hibiscus house I had filled dozens of journals with the details of my days and thoughts. I had started writing them as a way of keeping a connection to my friend Natasha, who had died when she was twenty and I nineteen. We had met by exchanging our zines through the post and from this formed a strong bond. Our identities merged to the point at which sometimes I felt more like her than myself. She had been the one to keep journals, sitting cross-legged on her bed bending intently over her notebook, writing across the pages in wide, unruly script, ignoring the blue-ruled lines.

After she died I spent a week with her parents and we began to sort her belongings. She had grown up on a farm, six hours' drive from where I lived in the city. There was little distraction for my heavy heart amid the flat fields. In our callowness Natasha and I had spoken of our delight in the 'dead people's clothes' in the country-town op shop, and had bought armfuls of black lace dresses and velvet coats. I no longer felt so invulnerable when I encountered these clothes again without her.

I brought home a suitcase of clothes and a blank notebook I had found among her papers, of the same kind as those she had kept her journals in, A4 with a red and blue cardboard cover with a paisley pattern. She would have filled these pages, had she lived. I felt her hand overlapping mine as I opened it and wrote in the date. I started with a sentence that had been ringing in my head, from the local newspaper article that had announced her death: *The talented musician had dreamed of becoming a writer.* Unlike me, she'd had clear intentions, and now that I lived for both of us I took up the journal in her stead.

The journals have continued through thousands of pages, thousands of days. There are as many of them on my bookshelf as there had been *National Geographic*s when I went looking for butterflies in them as a child. That time feels both immediate and remote. Sometimes it is present, other times it recedes, as I drift with, or resist, the circumstances that push me onwards.

Animal Chronicle I

Life in a Rotten Log
LIFE IN A ROTTEN LOG
Kathie Atkinson
THE CHILDREN'S BOOK COUNCIL
EVE POWELL AWARD
Kathie Atkinson

Animal Chronicle I

Come and look, I hear Simon call, his voice insistent, so I walk through the gloom of the house until I reach the doorway where I blink, dazzled by the daylight for a moment. Then his shape resolves, standing by the fence, pointing. Three brown beetles, big as acorns, with feathered antennae, are hovering around the front gate. Their wings buzz like motors as they work to keep their bulky bodies airborne.

The gate around which they are flying hangs crookedly. Every year it sits more askew, dislodged by the thick roots of the roadside row of fig trees. People passing by register the gate and the dilapidated house behind it as if it is a bad omen, disrupting the order of the street. The house's disrepair makes humans nervous but animals are drawn to it: cats shelter in its foundations, possums push through into the roof, spiders dwell in the splintered wood of the window frames.

The beetles are attracted to a crack between the pavement and the footings of the gate, where a seam of earth has been exposed. They descend to it like helicopters coming in to land. Immediately they begin to excavate. With strong movements of their front legs they push away dirt and twigs, intent on burrowing under the surface.

We watch their steadfast digging. They are frantic to embed themselves but the fissure is shallow, the earth compacted by the concrete and the tree roots. Even so, they continue to tunnel, persisting for so long that their determination outlasts our patience and we retreat inside the house. Later I imagine them down inside the earth, like seeds.

—

Amid the daily news was the story of Knickers, a gigantic steer twice as big as the cattle he grazes with. A photograph presented the steer's oversized black-and-white bulk amid the herd of brown cows, in which he has the look of a cruise ship moored in a harbour intended for smaller vessels.

I have come to the story late. It had first been reported two days before, enough time for it to distribute through world media. In the last forty-eight hours millions before me had read of the steer so large he would not fit in the abattoir machinery, and the farmer's quote: *He's too big for the chain.* Readers are left to imagine what the chain might be, although most will not think too deeply about it, and instead take the story of Knickers as a parable about the benefits of nonconformity. Knickers will live the rest of his days standing out from the herd, oblivious to the waning of his minor fame.

—

In one of the black plastic tubs of the cheapest used books for sale at the op shop is *Cat Catalog: The Ultimate Cat Book*. 'More than you ever imagined a cat book could be' is promised on the back cover, and I can't dispute this claim. Within the 345 pages are articles on cats across cultures, in art and literature, cat shows, cat genetics, acupuncture for cats, the politics of strays, psychic cats and a calico cat needlepoint pattern. I turn to a page at random and find out that in terms of their nutritional needs, cats can be considered undersized lions. On the next page I read about artist Utagawa Kuniyoshi's 'cat alphabets'. On the page following this is a diagram of the correct hold to restrain a cat in order to give it a pill.

Flicking through all this is more than enough to convince me that it is worth the two dollars to examine it further. The book was published in the 1970s and is inscribed on the flyleaf *From the library of Diana Gray*, with a sticker of a grey-striped Manx cat with yellow eyes affixed underneath. Now that the book has come to me by the serendipitous method of op-shop donation I read the same words as Diana once must have. How in ancient Egypt cats, with their ability to see in the dark, were thought to be magical. The cat goddess Bastet was a figure of worship, with dominion over the sun, moon, motherhood, love, protection of the dead and the success or failure of crops.

The description of ancient Egyptian cat funeral rites in this section is followed by a story from the nineteenth century. In 1888 tens of thousands of mummified cats were found buried in a cemetery near Beni-Hassan in Egypt. The cats were exhumed and their linen wrappings searched for gold and jewels. Then nineteen tonnes worth of them were shipped to England, and sold in Liverpool by an auctioneer who used a cat skull instead of an auction hammer for the occasion. The remains of these ancient cats were bought by farmers, who ground them up and used them as fertiliser on their fields.

I let the book go slack in my lap as I consider this scene. Night falls over the freshly tilled fields. The souls of the cats tangle in the soil, nocturnal and unquiet.

—

A millipede is curled up in the bathtub, a spiral against the pink enamel. Alive or dead, it's hard to tell, until I touch it and it unfurls. Skittering against the smooth surface, its frills of legs ripple. Its sudden appearance gives me the impression it has emanated from the cool darkness of the drain, like moths seem to arrive in a finger-click from the dusty air, and ants on the bench are pepper grounds come to life. The huntsman spiders that dart across the wall are like my dislodged thoughts and I chase after them with plastic containers, trying to trap them.

—

On the screen is an image of a dead tiger cub, curled with its paws over its eyes. I compel myself to look at it and a weight settles in my stomach as the image works through me. Its mother had died only a few days before she would have given birth. The cub came so close to life, only to be robbed of it by the poacher's snare. The people in the village near the forest in Sumatra where the tiger was trapped had heard her cries and alerted rangers, but by the time they reached her, it was too late.

I want to look away and forget. I want to look, bear witness, to this and the greater injustice it is a part of. As the article continues it explains how the forest habitat of the tiger is being replaced by plantations for palm oil, paper, and rubber. As I look over the list these substances seethe around me, the pantry dribbling palm oil, the papers dusty and yellowing on the shelves. The rubber soles of shoes sit heavy in the depths of the wardrobe. Outside, car tyres crackle over the road.

—

Beside the kitchen sink is a tall, wide drinking glass with a pattern of pastel stripes across its frosted surface. It must certainly be an illusion that water drunk from it seems sweeter and colder than from any other glass.

Reaching for it I notice the light catch on something at the rim, a silvery thread. I follow the thread across the mouth of the glass until I see the tiny spider that has produced it. The spider is so small it is barely anything at all, a white dot, half the size of a pinhead or less. I bring the glass up to the light, see the web spun neatly across it, and how the spider sits in the middle of this web as if it is the centre of the world.

—

The pedestrian tunnel that leads out from Central railway station surges with people. The fastest weave in and out, advancing with a swerving forward momentum. Slower walkers stick to the edges of the tunnel, near the seam of the wall where the leaves and gum wrappers accumulate in the gutter below the yellow tiles. Here at the slow edge I fall into step behind a man and a boy walking together. The man has tattooed arms, the left inscribed with a trail of playing cards, the right with tentacles and an anchor, a scroll with a name, and a row of gemstones leading down to his hand, which is holding the hand of the boy. The boy is eight or so, has the same angular face as the man, and on one arm has shapes drawn in red marker as if he yearns for his own cards and tentacles to decorate his skin.

Did you know I'm an owl, the man says, in a mild tone of voice as if he is making an observation of the weather or the crowd. I suspect I have misheard this weird utterance but then the boy replies, *Did you know I'm a panda,* and I realise they are playing a game. The man continues, *Did you know I'm a quokka,* and the boy replies, *Did you know I'm a rat,* and the man says, *Did you know I'm a snake,* and the boy asks, *Did you know I'm a Tasmanian Devil?* The man says *no, I didn't know that, I didn't know that at all.* He must be stalling for time, trying to think of an animal starting with U. The end of the tunnel is in sight, a flare of light opening to the sky, as the man says, *Did you know I'm a unicorn?*

—

The sky is patterned by wisps of cloud that look like dissipating letters, lost messages. This sets my attention whirring, unable to settle on any one detail until I reach the park and see the man standing in the centre of the lawn, looking down. He stares at the grass near where he has set a portable speaker. The heavy guitar rock emitting from it comes across as a high-pitched whine, but it is not this he is inspecting. He advances a few steps and picks something up. It's a turtle, which pokes its head out from its shell, and waves its feet around with the surprise of being suddenly airborne.

I stop to talk to him and he tells me the story of the turtle. One of his friends had come across it when cutting grass for the council, the man says. He explains how there is a group of people who go into swamplands to rescue turtles when these lands are drained for new developments. I tell you, these developers are fucking up the place, he says, as he puts the turtle back down on the grass.

At home I sit on the front step while the black cat rolls on the pebblecrete beside me, wriggling back and forwards then sitting up, shaking so puffs of dust come off into the air like she's in a cartoon. She looks at me with pale green eyes and blinks and I blink slowly in return. The *Cat Catalog* has taught me that this is how cats express affection. I feel love for this stray that has chosen me, for turtles and the people who rescue them, for the clouds above, for everything that is contained in this moment.

—

In the waiting room there is a tissue box on the table printed with an image of two pandas, which float within an indistinct green background, with the caption 'Animal Paradise'. This design is repeated over the six sides of the box to create a world in which they only ever encounter themselves.

This mundane surrealism triggers a string of associations: pandas reared in captivity being introduced to the wild by humans wearing panda suits; a Jehovah's Witness pamphlet promising 'Life in a Peaceful New World' illustrated by a painting of children tumbling with pandas; an op-shop T-shirt I bought on a day when an unexpected flare of hot weather made me desperate for short sleeves. It was printed with a cartoon of a panda wearing a striped shirt and a beret and holding up a camera, under the word 'Bonjour'. I had felt ridiculous wearing it, like an overgrown child.

Then I think of visiting Bao Bao the giant panda at the Berlin Zoo, approaching the long window behind which he was sitting, close to the glass. Bao Bao and I had been born in the same year, I noted from the information that was presented on the nearby panel, which meant that he too was approaching his thirtieth birthday. I tried to draw some significance from this connection, but it was difficult to imagine our life stories side by side in any meaningful way. Thirty was old for a panda. I was still working out what life as a human was all about.

—

It is evening, the light low and greyish in this narrow back street, where the houses crowd together in rows, and cars are parked tightly, only inches to spare around them. A ginger cat runs across the street ahead of me, low to the ground, something in its mouth which initially I think is a bird, but then see is a crumbed cutlet, as if it has just stolen it from a dinner plate. It slinks into the dark cave underneath a parked car with its prize.

At the end of the street a blue gum tree contains a chorus of lorikeets. The cacophony has an elusive melody, constantly escaping, fracturing into a tumbling ball of sound that blanks out everything else. There must be many dozens of birds in the tree to produce such an intensity of sound, but as closely as I look, I cannot see even one of them. They are hidden by the leaves shadowed in the dusk, as they cluster and depose each other from branches, calling out that the day is over.

The tree is a twittering machine, exploding with raucous life. I stop to observe it and the sound vibrates through me. I decide I won't move on until I see at least one bird. My eyes tangle in the leaves and branches. Finally a lorikeet appears, flying in, a blue-green flash, quickly absorbed by the foliage.

—

In the guttering above the barber shop a bird is having a bath, fluttering in a shallow pool of rainwater left after the morning's storm. The sun has come out again and the droplets sparkle as they splash up from the gutter. It's hard to tell what kind of bird it is amid the flurry of wings and water but when it does hop up to the tiles, I see that it is a common myna, brown and black with a yellow beak. Its wet feathers stick together in spikes that give it the bratty look of a punk, striding over the tiled awning on its thin, yellow legs as if on a stage.

I'd hoped it to be a different bird than the ubiquitous, bullying myna. Mynas are a pest species, an aggressive competitor with native birds, after being introduced to Australia in the nineteenth century to control insects in crop fields. Soon it became evident that, rather than eating the caterpillars they had been brought in to control, the mynas far preferred to eat the produce itself, pecking into the fruits and grains the farmers had hoped to protect.

The myna hops up on the railing of the balcony above, then onto a towel stretched across a wire rack, and continues to ruffle its feathers. A minute later a woman appears at the balcony door. She looks out over the street below before noticing the bird. She watches it, smiling at how the bird continues to ruffle its feathers, unbothered by her presence. But then she cannot resist the urge to move it along and she stretches forward, sweeping her hand to shoo it away.

—

When I go out walking I follow the riverside path or zigzag through the suburban streets. People rarely pay me much attention unless the dogs are with me. A greyhound and a whippet are a conspicuous pair and people are keen to ask me about them. They're my sister's dogs, I explain, but I borrow them sometimes.

I clip their leads to their collars, let them pull me out the gate. The path is wet and fresh after rain and I stand waiting while the greyhound Luisa moves her nose – her *gomme*, Fiona and I call it, for its resemblance to a pencil eraser – over the base of a tree trunk, reading it thoroughly. Her investigation takes a long time and as I stand waiting a man comes up and stops beside us.

Greyhound, he says, indicating Luisa at the tree, where she continues sniffing, intent on whatever canine information it is revealing. The man turns to Laszlo at the end of the other lead and furrows his brow in mock-contemplation. Whippet?

You pass the test, I say, as I do every time this scene occurs. He laughs, then turns back to Luisa. Ex-racer? he asks. This too is a frequent question.

In the course of Fiona's work for a greyhound rescue organisation she had found the finish-line photograph from the race in which Luisa had come first. A black streak, legs extended, a body-length ahead of the other dogs. She only ran two races before she was surrendered to the pound. In this she was more fortunate than most racing dogs. I knew the kinds of things that happened to these dogs, kept them in mind for when people wanted to tell me that greyhound racing was harmless.

Yes, I say, she's a rescue dog. The man nods and reaches over to pat Luisa, scratching her behind the ear inside which her racing number is tattooed. At this point the conversation can go one of two ways and I can't quite guess where this man's sympathies reside. Luisa lifts her head from the tree trunk and moves closer to him, drawn by his affection. That's right, the man says, you're safe from that cruel world. Things are better now.

—

Life in a
Rotten
Log

A children's book, ex-library, old enough to have a card in a pocket on the inside cover and a date-due slip. No dates are stamped on it, and the card is blank apart from the book's name and call number, showing no borrowers although it was published twenty-five years ago. It has waited a long time for its intended recipient. I take the book from where it is housed beside the unpopular novels and outmoded cookbooks in the cabinet of free books at the train station, and bring it home with me.

I have other tasks to attend to, more pressing than the reading of a children's book on forest ecology, but the topic of the rotten log draws me in.

The first thing to note about the rotten log is that it is a busy place. The inhabitants, some of them soft, others armoured, take up residence within the decomposing mass of the log. They slither and creep, some predators, others prey. Some have long tongues, others have sharp claws. Blind white termites chew through the softening wood. Yellow slime mould advances over it in creeping threads, as it digests the bacteria that are in turn feeding on the wood. Rot is a complicated, collective business.

Among the photographs I am drawn to a soft grey centipede-like animal known as the velvet worm. The caption explains its alternative name is *Peripatus*, although from the image it doesn't appear as if it would be such an effective wanderer, with its row of blunt legs that look like soft, fat loops of wool. At night it emerges from the log to search for the beetles and crickets that are its sustenance. It would seem there would be no chance of the sluggish velvet worm overpowering such insects, yet it targets them and shoots out a slime that glues them down, fixing them on the spot so that it has time to lumber over and consume them. All through the rotten log, such scenes of life and death play out.

—

In the loading dock at the back of the shopping centre three cockatoos are perched on top of a tower of brown plastic bread trays. Each is holding a crust of bread, which they have nibbled into irregular shapes, so they seem to be holding alphabet letters as they peer down at me. They have been interrupted by my arrival and are now paused, waiting for my next move. When I don't make any attempt to chase them away, they turn back down to their crusts, working at them with their tough grey beaks and blunt tongues.

The shopping centre is a behemoth of a building which grows every year, spreading further up or out into another block of windowless rendered concrete. I rarely enter it but cross the car park as a shortcut, walking past the service entries, the bins and the loading dock. This is the grimy, hidden part of the complex, where goods are received and waste is removed. Sometimes people who work in the centre sit on the loading dock on their breaks, smoking or looking at their phones, amid the trash and bollards, thankful to be somewhere quiet and unobserved.

I leave the birds to their picnic and walk on. Later, when I hear a flock of white cockatoos overhead, I imagine the harsh rasps of their voices are tearing the air, like their claws tore through the plastic bags around the loaves of bread. The sound of their cries momentarily blanks out all else, as I stand below them, earthbound.

—

There are quiet places to retreat to in the city, you just have to know where to find them. Entering the low-ceilinged shopping arcade, I turn down a corridor to the side which leads to the secret garden. Two storeys above street level, at the foot of an office tower, the garden has tall trees, a palm grove, beds of agapanthus, and a pond which is home to a school of white and orange carp.

I walk up to the edge of it and they come swirling over, kissing the water's surface, hoping for crumbs. Opening my notebook

I write in the date and underline it, then look back down at the carp, which cluster at the water's surface below me, waiting for something to come to them. *What words are to me, crumbs are to them*, I think, as I turn back to the page.

Mink Coat

Mink Coat

The camphorwood wardrobe was tall and heavy, a stern presence in the spare room at my grandparents' house. In every other room I liked to look through the drawers and cupboards, stickybeaking through the items that were tucked away from everyday use, but the wardrobe had a forbidding aura that repelled me. This was the kind of magic wardrobe that had led to Narnia, the kind that might swallow me into another dimension if I encountered it alone.

The only times I dared to look inside were when my mother or grandmother opened it to search for something within. The dresses and coats hanging on the rail seemed to be resting, thin ghosts waiting in the dark, with memories deeper than I had the years to fathom. These were clothes that had long passed out of fashion, suits and dresses that now appeared stiff and prim. All had once been worn by members of my family but took up fictional identities in my imagination. The tan trench coat could have been worn by a detective, and the blue woollen dress by a party hostess in a 1950s magazine advertisement. Boxes at the base of the wardrobe held slim, elegant shoes, made for demure steps.

At the end of the rail, pressed up against the side of the wardrobe, was a mink coat. It hung long and heavy with an animal weight, a broad shape with wide, padded shoulders, made up of vertical stripes of sleek fur, brown as chestnuts. Whenever the wardrobe was open my eyes went straight to it, and I'd ask my mother to again tell me its story.

It had belonged to my great-grandmother Sally, one of the few possessions she had brought with her when she came to Australia after the Second World War. Her family were Baghdadi Jews and, although she had been born in Iraq, she had lived for most of her life in treaty-port cities in China, first Hong Kong and then Shanghai. Unable to leave Shanghai before the war began, she had been confined in an internment camp with other foreign nationals. After her release she left for Australia and travelled to the country town of Armidale where her daughter – my grandmother – lived with her husband and two small children, one of whom was my mother.

The first time my mother met Sally was at Armidale station, after the arrival of Sally's train from Sydney. On the platform Sally stood waiting, wearing the mink coat, with her long hair wound up onto the crown of her head. My mother, a child then, had been shy at the sight of this elegant woman, who seemed to be from another world entirely, starkly different to that of the country town to which she had come. I never tired of hearing this story. When my mother described my great-grandmother I imagined myself in the story too, sometimes looking on shyly with my mother, at other times as Sally herself, standing on the platform, my coils of hair heavy on my head, hot inside my long coat.

Sally had died three years before I was born, but sometimes my mother would show me the black-and-white passport photo of her that she kept in a silver frame and say, 'See how she looks like you? You have the same gentle spirit as her.' Looking at the photograph I felt the outline of her face within my own, the same dark eyes and slight smile. Through our physical resemblance I sensed that I carried something of her character with me. This was a coat of a different kind, one offering intrinsic protection, one that cannot be taken off and set aside.

The mink coat itself horrified and fascinated me. The fur was very soft, so much so that my hand seemed to melt into it when

I touched it. Instinctively I would stroke it as if it were alive. From the size of the coat I imagined a mink must be a large animal, huge as a bear. Somehow I worked out that it was otherwise, and that minks were the size of cats, and the coat was made of the skins of many mink pelts stitched together. Fifty or sixty minks would have died to make a coat of this kind and this level of sacrifice made me wary. I'd seen the anti-fur protests on the news, the footage of blood-red paint being thrown over the shop windows of New York furriers and, it was said, over people who went out wearing fur coats in public. In my child's understanding of it I believed Sally's coat to be something it would be wisest to keep secret.

I developed a fascination with this woman whom I could never meet, but who I carried within me as a source of inner strength. My mother brought her to me through her memories. Throughout my mother's teenage years they had shared a room, so I knew how Sally would read prayers every night before sleep, then kiss the book and slip it under her pillow before turning off the light. The prayer book was small and worn, and the Hebrew text on the thin pages seemed to my uncomprehending eyes a dance of dots and dashes. The facts of Sally's life were equally remote. She had been born in Hillah, Iraq, a few years before the turn of the twentieth century. Then her family moved to Hong Kong where she married and had two children, one of whom was my grandmother. It was difficult to imagine these as real events. My grandmother was elderly and moved slowly, restricted by arthritis. Mostly she could be found in the kitchen, a comforting figure in a floral-patterned dress and apron who gave me Milky Way chocolate bars from a reserve that she kept in a high-up cupboard. I struggled to envisage her as a child like me, let alone imagine the generations before her.

When the Gulf War began in 1990 I saw Iraq on the television, in grey-green night-vision landscapes, lit up by explosions. I was convinced this conflict signalled a third world war. I had grown up with my grandparents' stories of the Second World War, still so present in their memories, and so it seemed likely that there would be a war of the same scale that it would be my experience to live through. This merged with my childhood fears of nuclear attack, and I listened to the radio reports of the Gulf War incessantly, unable to settle back into my usual activities, waiting for the cataclysmic moment that signalled the end of the world. Early the next year when the retreating Iraqi forces set hundreds of Kuwaiti oil wells on fire, the television showed images of plumes of flame and black smoke rising out of the desert. Although it marked the end of the war, there was little relief in the apocalyptic vision of the burning desert.

Another decade on came the 2003 invasion of Iraq by the United States, supported by a coalition that included Australia. Older now, my response was more disgust than terror, that war was being staged in the name of the country of which I was a citizen. One day during this time, watching the television news with its footage of armoured vehicles and broken buildings, I noticed that the location given at the base of the screen was Hillah. Much time, history and change had passed since my great-grandmother had been born there, but still, a thread connected me.

The city is south of Baghdad, adjacent to the ruins of Babylon. In the late nineteenth century, around the time Sally was born, German archaeologists were on the site of the ancient city, making excavations of glazed brick tiles. It was the era of colonial plunder. European museums were stocked with objects from such excavations, devotional, grand or mundane things, forming material evidence of human history that the colonial powers believed it was their right to take. Outside Hillah the more the excavators dug the more they found, eventually uncovering the remains of one of the city's walls, made of blue and green glazed tiles decorated by lions, bulls and dragons. Tens of thousands of fragments from the wall were removed to Europe, and then, over years, pieced together like an immense jigsaw.

The wall had been built during the reign of Nebuchadnezzar, the king of Babylon in the sixth century BCE. His name has been branded on my memory from a moment in a primary school religion class, when one of the questions on a quiz had been how to spell it. The teacher read out the question and the girl sitting beside me went pale at the thought of attempting it. I moved my hand so that she could copy my answer, confident in my knowledge of how the word fitted together. The trick to remembering it was to break it up into pieces, then stick it back together again on the page.

This memory flickered back to me when, as an adult, I stood in the Pergamon Museum in Berlin, at the foot of the reconstructed wall, named the Ishtar Gate after the Babylonian goddess of love and war. It is a monumental structure, five storeys high, walls of bright blue tiles with yellow borders. Across the two walls on either side of the arch are rows of animals in bas-relief: a string of wild bulls with curled horns, then a row of dragons with snake heads and scorpion tails. The animals are neatly arrayed, subdued by the structure of the wall and, by inference, the king's power, as well as invoking the gods they represented. A processional walkway, decorated with snarling lions, leads the way towards the gate within.

My favourite of the animals on the tiles was the dragon, the sirrush, a mixture of reptile, bird and mammal. It wore a look of purpose in its beady snake's eye as it strode forward on its mismatched legs, two of a lion, two of an eagle. It was a patchwork creature, a compilation of ferocious qualities, brought together into one organism.

Looking up at the sirrush, I am the woman with long hair, wearing a grey dress, standing in front of the Ishtar Gate. I'm also the girl who had watched the Gulf War on the television. I am my mother opening the wardrobe door and telling me about her grandmother's coat, I am my grandmother in a floral dress taking a chocolate bar from the cupboard, I am my great-grandmother in the mink coat on the railway platform, as I am the women from the generations before her, whose identities I will never know.

—

Before I came to live there in my twenties I'd never been in my grandparents' house by myself. By this time my grandparents had died, and until their house was sold I was to live there as its caretaker. It was sparser than I had ever known it, the brown flocked wallpaper replaced by white paint and most of the heavy, old furniture removed to make the house a blank canvas for potential buyers to imagine their own lives upon.

On my first day alone there, space and silence settled around me. The coming months would be my time to absorb the last of the house's comfort. I unpacked my boxes of books and papers, set up my desk, boiled the kettle for tea, and sat on the back step looking out at the yard. The vegetable gardens were empty apart from the plum and grapefruit trees, but the strelitzia flowers were in bloom, their bird-like heads emerging from long green stems. The pock of tennis balls echoed from the courts in the park behind the house. Magpies sung from the park's tall eucalyptus trees. These sounds wrapped around me like a soft, well-worn fabric.

It wasn't until later that night that I opened the sliding door to the spare room at the side of the house. It was an extension that had been built after the house itself, and had a more provisional, tangential atmosphere than the other rooms. The patterned amber glass of the door yellowed the light, and a carpeted step led down into it. The boards were smooth, my footsteps echoed. The room had been a workshop for my grandfather for a while, then a bedroom for my mother and sister, but now it was almost empty. The only furniture that remained in it was the camphorwood wardrobe. Too solid to move, it was in the same place as ever, stout and serious, as if protesting the changes that were occurring around it.

With my fingers gripping the handle of the wardrobe door I pressed in the metal button that released the latch. When I took my hand away the door swung open, its creak a distinctive voice. At first I thought the wardrobe to be empty. Most of the clothes and shoes that used to be stored there had been cleared out, donated to op shops or given away. As my eyes adjusted to the wardrobe's depths, though, I saw it. In its usual position, at the end of the railing, the mink coat.

It was as soft as I remembered. As I leaned into the wardrobe further the door creaked again and I looked over my shoulder. There was nothing there, just the louvre windows and the night outside, but I thought of my grandmother telling me how Sally had appeared in her dreams in times of difficulty or struggle.

She would be sitting on the end of my grandmother's bed, sometimes speaking, other times not, as real as if she had been alive. I shook off the thought and took the coat out of the closet. It had a musty, organic smell that clung to me as I slipped one arm into it, then the other. It was heavy on my shoulders and I immediately felt the uncomfortable warmth of the fur in the humid summer night.

As I settled my body into the coat a movement caught my eye. Now there was someone there. She was reflected in the mirror on the inside of the wardrobe door. A woman with long hair and dark eyes, wearing a mink coat, her face familiar and strange.

Glass Fish

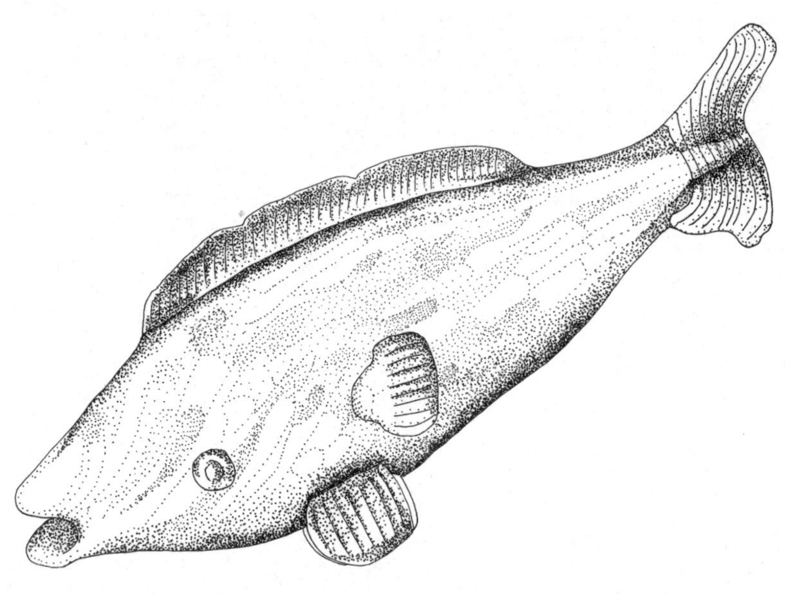

Glass Fish

In my room, sitting at my desk, I feel as secret as a yolk. My shell is the four walls, painted in a shade called 'Phantom Dream', although it is a bland off-white that provokes no such fantasy. The walls have postcards and pictures stuck to them and blank patches are marked with Blu-Tack stains where cards have been taken down and not replaced by new ones. Chips in the paint reveal glimpses of a previous layer, a pale pink memory.

The room can take me elsewhere as much as contain me. The carpet, patterned with purple ripples, seems to move like the shallows of a river, taking me along with its tide. The window is an eye out to an oak tree with leaves that tremble even on breezeless days. High up on the wall, through the lattice of the air vent, the room breathes. Suspended at the end of a cord in the centre of the ceiling is a pink glass lightshade that collects the husks of the insects which are drawn into its glow.

The room is at the back of the house, in the corner of the lot, at the end of the road before it reaches the railway line. The room is a centre around which other things move. Freight trains run all day and night. Planes ascend from the airport in the east, angling up and away. Closer are the ibis, soaring over with their white wings outstretched. In the evening flying foxes cross the sky in a steady procession of black shapes, like pieces of dislodged night.

The room has its own menagerie: a polystyrene bear a metre tall and painted glitter silver; a ceramic crocodile small as a fingernail; a long, blue-black raven tailfeather; a ball of soft grey fur from a pet rabbit; a collection of cicada shells, a woodblock print of a cat sitting on a windowsill; a glass fish with a swirl of colour in its belly.

The fish travelled here in the centre of a suitcase, cushioned by winter clothes, floating within layers of bubble wrap. When the tape that secured it was unpeeled, the touch of the antique dealer who had wrapped it fluttered around the room like a moth, farewelling the fish into a new sea.

The room is for dreaming in and writing in and other, secondary purposes which cluster like minnows. It is for this reason I acquired the glass fish. It moves through the school of small concerns, a charm of serene focus.

The room is cluttered but there is always space for more things. Moving books and ornaments aside, I place the fish at the centre of the shelf.

Here, the fish carries my reflection.

The room contains twenty years of my life in four dozen notebooks, stacked up on the shelf guarded by the fish.

Whether I am in it or not, the room is animated. Each day the light moves across the window, casting the branches outside in shadows on the wall. Before I came to live here, other people observed this same cycle.

The room has been the room of a musician, containing a tower of speakers and equipment. Before that it was the spare room of the woman who planted the snowdrops which bloom every spring in the garden. She thought of it as the baby's room, although she had no children.

The fish retains the impressions of past rooms it has been in. The family's lounge room where it decorated the top of a television, resting on a lace doily. When the mother's eyes strayed from the screen she saw herself reflected, small and distorted, in its glass belly. She sold it to an antique store, and it was there I had spied it, displayed beside a metal screen shaped like a peacock's tail.

The room holds many other rooms inside of it: an infinite regress of rooms, tunnelling through space and time. The rooms I have entered, slept in, thought of as mine. The rooms that all the objects have been through before ending up here. The rooms described in the books on the shelves: Gregor Samsa hiding behind the closed door of his room; Antoinette Cosway in her attic, dreaming of the house burning.

The room will disappear. Its objects will be packed away, the lost things that had slipped down behind the bookcases will be retrieved, the furniture will be carried out. The room will look smaller than it seemed the whole time I knew it. I will look out the window at the oak tree one final time before turning away, leaving the house empty. The excavator will take a first bite, then another, opening up the side wall. Then the house will be gone, its space returned to the open air.

The room keeps me safe, I rarely want to leave it. As in a spell, it is a circle drawn around me. The circle is a clock face which I chase the hands around. It is a wheel which carries my life as it spins. The circle is a lake, inside which I float. Reeds brush up against me, obscuring the view so the depth of the waters beneath is difficult to fathom. Within the lake a seam of cool water comes with a stirring, the movement of a shape I recognise. The fish, aswim beside me.

Rabbit Island

Rabbit Island

A ferry pulls in at the jetty at Tadanoumi, accompanied by a waft of exhaust fumes. We board it and step into a cabin decorated in pastel tones like a baby's bedroom, the seats upholstered in pale blue vinyl, the scuffed linoleum floor patterned with pink rainbows. A clock with silver hands ticks out the time on the laminate wall. Underneath it are notices, printed pages stating the timetable and evacuation procedures, and a laminated photograph of three brown and white rabbits.

The ferry idles, waiting for more passengers. There are only five of us on board apart from the ferry master and the deckhand. Simon and I sit on one side of the cabin, across from two young women who are busy peering into their pocket mirrors, blotting their faces with slips of tissue paper. Outside on deck the fifth passenger, a man in a suit, sits looking over the water. The boat sways at anchor. No one else arrives and after five minutes the deckhand unmoors the ferry and we begin the journey.

On a summer day like this, mid-morning, there would usually be more passengers. The ferry's destination, the island of Ōkunoshima, is a popular tourist destination. There are only a few structures on the island – a resort hotel, the ruins of a poison gas factory, and a museum – but it is not for this that most of the visitors come. The island is a novelty for being a rabbit sanctuary and tourists visit daily, bringing carrots and lettuce to feed them. The most popular explanation for the rabbits on the island is that they had been laboratory animals that were set free after the factory was closed in 1945, a story neat but false. The rabbits were introduced to the island decades later, after it had already been turned over to recreation, and then proliferated to a point where they became the island's distinguishing feature.

The lack of people was not just noticeable on the ferry to Ōkunoshima. There was an eerie mood of depopulation everywhere we went: at train stations and at tourist sites, in the sparsely occupied parking lots and in the dispersed, scattered groupings of people in thoroughfares that had been designed for crowds. It was only three months after the Fukushima nuclear accident and although the reactor was far to the north, the extent of the contamination was feared throughout Japan. The accident, caused by a flood after the Tōhoku earthquake and tsunami, had made people cautious and reticent to travel.

That morning in Kyoto we had walked alongside a protest march, a crowd of people holding yellow placards, calling for a nuclear-free future. Japan has dozens of nuclear reactors inside numerous power stations, which at the time of the accident had accounted for around a third of the country's electricity. In the aftermath the operating reactors were gradually being shut down, but only temporarily, despite public opinion being strongly against their reactivation.

Through the window of the ferry I can see the island in the near distance, a ripple of dense green hills with a tall metal pylon on its northernmost side. Wires stretch out from it, drooping over towards the next pylon, linking the island to the mainland. The network of powerlines that extend across the country, overlaying the landscape, had surprised me. Pylons are omnipresent, city or country, spiking up from mountains, lurking in valleys, clinging to cliffsides. The pylon on Ōkunoshima, at over 200 metres tall, is the highest in all of Japan, providing the island with another unlikely claim to notoriety.

As I watch, the island enlarges, dark green forest and the sandy scallops of beaches coming into sharper focus the closer we get. Soon the boat slows to pull in at the wharf. In the otherwise empty parking lot is a minibus, and in front of it stands a man wearing a white shirt tucked into black trousers, who gestures between me and the bus with enthusiastic sweeps of his arms. I try to convey that we are not the people for whom he has been waiting. He indicates that we are making a mistake. Our exchange is interrupted by the man in the suit from the deck, the rightful passenger.

They leave in the minibus and now the road is without vehicles, as the picnic tables underneath the brick-and-tile shelters are without picnickers. The two young women walk ahead onto one of the paths, the ferry pulls away, and quickly there's no one else around but us. The humid weather gives the scene a languid haze, in which time seems to stagnate.

We move towards the shade at the edge of the trees and a group of rabbits emerge, loping their way out of the shadows. They are a ragged, lean troupe, in varying shades of brown and black, who hop up close to us and perch on their back legs, awaiting food. I immediately realise the paucity of my offering. I'd brought two carrots I'd purchased from a convenience store, individually wrapped in cellophane bags. A gold ribbon tied the wrapping at the top of each, as if they were special gifts. Without exception all the fruit and vegetables in the store had been packaged like this, with the same ceremonial appearance, swathed in plastic. The effect on me had been twofold. Along with noting the wastefulness of its overpackaging came an intensified scrutiny of the vegetable within.

The rabbits know well the crackle and rustle of plastic bags. As I sit on a bench to untie the ribbon on the first package some jump up on my lap, while the rest mill around my legs. I hadn't expected them to be so assertive. Wild rabbits typically flee from any sudden movements or approaches by humans. Their survival is based on their ability to detect danger and escape from it. Here however little threatens them, and they rely on tourists with carrots to feed them. They are lean and insistent as they cluster around me.

In Australia rabbits are an introduced pest species responsible for environmental degradation on a grand scale, and so for me to be surrounded by them is something of a dystopian scene. The rabbits paw at me, desperate for slivers of carrot. They're cute in a lean, soft, big-eyed way, yet I can't help but think of footage of rabbit plagues in the outback, or of *Night of the Lepus,* the only horror film I've seen, maybe the only horror film that exists, with rabbits as the monsters. Predictably this B-grade film fails to present this convincingly. Their real-life menace comes instead with their ability to multiply, with the sharp dig of their claws into the soil and their collective, herbivorous hunger.

For many years I'd had one as a pet. A friend had seen a black rabbit running free in her local dog park and rescued it, and then sent a message around to see if anyone wanted to take him in. Although I knew next to nothing about keeping rabbits, the long ears and alert eyes of the one in the picture hinted at a watchful, attentive character, and I wrote back to say yes, I would take him.

I soon came to know that for many people a rabbit is not considered to be a very adult pet. More often than I expected, people would make jokes about eating him, expressing a delight in pointing out that my pet was edible that was difficult for me to understand. Having been a vegetarian for decades I made little distinction between food animals and companion animals, in terms of what kind of soul they might or might not have. If called on to explain my choice of pet I described my rabbit as my familiar. He always seemed to be busy or in mid-thought, doing his own thing as I did mine. I'd sit out in the yard, writing or reading, and look up now and then to see him nibbling or digging or preening inside his wire enclosure, ever alert to sounds or movements that could signal potential disruption or danger.

On nights when the moon is full a rabbit watches over the earth from above, its shape visible in the pattern of craters on the moon's surface. Once I saw the moon this way I could no longer see it otherwise. In Japanese legends the moon rabbit is busy with a mortar and pestle, grinding rice flour to make mochi cakes; in Chinese legends the same rabbit mixes up the elixir of life. The busy energies of the rabbit, which can cause such destruction, are in these interpretations a creative, protective force.

I scatter the rest of the carrot and we move onwards, towards a set of grey ruins, the remains of a power station, its concrete exterior covered by the tracings of dead vines. The rusted window frames hang askew and only a few broken panes of glass are left in them to catch the light. Once this building powered the island's factories. During the 1930s Ōkunoshima was the centre of chemical weapons manufacture in Japan. In this era it was omitted from maps and its deadly industry, producing mustard and tear gas for the Sino-Japanese war, continued in secret.

Histories link up, thread through to my own. The Japanese invasion of China was a turning point in my family history, as my grandparents fled Shanghai ahead of the arrival of Japanese troops. We had to leave everything we had behind, my grandmother told me, still with sadness, fifty years afterwards. Only later, as an adult, I realised that her sorrow was for more than the objects in their apartment. It was for a life she would never return to. When she spoke of that time I knew there was only so far I could travel with her, only so far my imagination could peel away the present-day, suburban surroundings in which we lived together.

Here on Ōkunoshima rabbits rest in the shade of the ruins, under trees, and on the sparse lawns. Behind a stand of palm trees is a hotel, the only business on the island. A few vans are parked nearby, packed full of boxes containing miscellaneous items, including a large wall clock which pokes up askew. In front of the hotel are the two women from the boat, one feeding a lettuce leaf to three brown baby rabbits as the other holds up her phone, recording the scene.

Everywhere we pause rabbits hop up to us, so I slice up half of the second carrot into wedges and scatter these like crumbs to pigeons. This distracts some of them while I hold onto the remainder of the carrot, and the rest cluster around in a frenzy. The rabbits take big, toothy crunches as they jostle for the best position. Quickly they reduce the carrot to a stump, and I have to drop it for the sake of my fingers. I look up towards the power stanchions and the electricity cables that stretch out across the grid. Follow them far enough north and I would come to Fukushima and the leaking reactor, and that deserted city with its starving, roaming pets, abandoned in the evacuation.

I follow another thought-path, one that travels south, over the ocean and across the vast continent I live at the eastern edge of.

I imagine looking over the desert through the plane window, down to where in the west there runs the rabbit-proof fence, thousands of kilometres long. Here rabbits have overgrazed the land, eroded it and made it barren, starving out other species. My thought-path continues, comes down to land, to the suburban garden where my own rabbit lives, housed in a long enclosure under the shade of an elm tree.

This rabbit I know as an individual with a life story and a distinct character. On the night I return home I go out to the yard to look up at the moon. The mochi-pounding rabbit is busy above, and when I raise my hand to the wire mesh at my side, the rabbit's whiskers and warm breath are on my fingers as he comes over to greet me, a sensation only just perceptible, as mild as the moonlight which beams down upon us.

Frank the Bear

KODIAK BEAR
FRANK

Frank the Bear

Inside the biology museum the walls were painted bright red, and the rows of glass cabinets encased specimens of different orders of animals. One cabinet contained trays of insects, another held specimens of lizards, and others held taxidermy mammals and marsupials, posed as if alive, possums and gliders paused on branches mid-climb. Affixed at eye-level along one wall was a series of bulbous perspex hemispheres, each of which contained an owl. In a corner display case was a human skeleton seated on a red stool. The skeleton and I were the only human presences in this dimly lit room which smelt faintly of chemicals and hummed with the sound of the fluorescent lights that illuminated the displays.

It was a small museum, housing the university's teaching collection, and although I had never seen anyone else in there, every so often there were new names and comments written in the visitors' book on the table by the door. Kids left succinct reviews of the museum declaring it 'cool', or 'weird', or that it had a 'funny smell'. Flipping the pages back I found my own name, in an entry dated the year before. Coming across my handwriting was like recognising a face in a photograph then realising it to be my own. Beside my name was the comment 'Where's the Bear?' I still didn't know, and so I kept visiting the museum, in the hope I'd find out or the bear would return.

The bear was a memory that I'd come in search of. I had last visited the bear as a child, when I accompanied my grandfather on his visits to the university. He had worked in the physics department as a laboratory technician, and after he retired he ran a watch repair service through the campus newsagency. Every week he called in to pick up broken and stopped wristwatches and return those he had fixed. As his quietest and most studious grandchild I was deemed a suitable accomplice.

It seemed an act of great trust for people to leave their watches in our care. Unclasped from the wrists that wore them, the leather straps or metal links that made up the watch bands looked forlorn, as did the watches themselves, with their hands suspended at odd times, or with their digital displays blank. The exchange of the envelope of repaired watches for the envelope of those to fix seemed to me as solemn as a rite. Then, having received our weekly assignment, we went further within the maze of buildings that made up the campus to visit Frank the bear.

Frank was a Kodiak bear, taxidermically preserved in a standing posture inside a tall glass case with a wooden frame. His long, curved claws were at my eye level, and as I looked up to his broad chest and full height he seemed, from this aspect, to be immense. Yet I accepted his presence as not particularly out of the ordinary. My childhood world was populated by bears of all kinds, teddy bears and storybook bears, bears benevolent and sometimes sinister. So it didn't seem unusual that we were making these regular visits. Surely his being here at the university only meant that bears were as plentiful in adult life as they were in the lives of children.

I was certain Frank was on the verge of communicating something to me. I'd watch him through the glass, waiting for any sign of movement, a twitch of his claws, a stirring of his broad, furry torso. I was young enough to be under the thrall of fairytales, which gave every seemingly inanimate thing the potential to come to life, to be either friendly or menacing or both at once.

Frank was part of my own fairytale, set in the suburbs amid its landscape of highways, shopping malls and houses. My favourite places were those that didn't follow a predictable pattern, like the rivers and gullies and ribbons of bushland around which the streets were constructed, or the university with its cluster of brutalist buildings, as if it were one great grey fortress deconstructed into many parts. Every week an old man and a young girl entered the concrete maze to exchange offerings of wristwatches, and to make visits to Frank to ensure his ongoing protection. By keeping vigil over the biological sciences building Frank knew the secrets that were decoded within its laboratories.

In adolescence the characters in my story changed. Teddy bears and supernatural creatures were replaced by human figures, musicians who were the stars of different kinds of fairytales, in which the alchemical transformation of emotions into songs occurred. Coolness, disruption, subversion: these were my new influences. The bands had names and characters as vivid as those in storybooks – Siouxsie and the Banshees, X-Ray Spex, My Bloody Valentine – and in that way were a fitting progression from my childhood escapism, although not to my family as they observed how my guiding lights were changing, leading me towards rebellion.

With my black clothes and sullen demeanour, I worried my grandfather enough for him to write me a letter. He handed me an envelope with the instruction to open it when I was alone, and not be angry about the contents. The letter was written out by hand in the copperplate script he had learnt as a child in the 1920s. The thin, trailing lettering gave his message an oracular quality as he made predictions for my future. He cautioned me about the direction my life was taking, and urged me to respect my intelligence and gentle nature rather than give in to anger and sadness. He hoped I'd consider working as a teacher, but my future was up to me. 'Set a good course of your own choice,' he wrote. When I tried to imagine this future it seemed as blank as a strip of new cassette tape, shiny and inscrutable. I read the letter then hid it away, ashamed and resistant.

Decades later I came to work at the same university I had visited with my grandfather. I had grown up, and he had passed away, but the university had changed very little, the maze of concrete buildings as confusing to navigate as before. This was my first time teaching, tutoring undergraduate students in creative writing. In the classes I instructed my students to be precise in their language and careful with their research, coaching them through the observational exercises about places and people that novice writers are routinely given. Afterwards I retreated to the staff room on the top level of the arts building, with its giant tin of Nescafé and copies of the *Paris Review*, relieved that the classes had proceeded without disaster.

One day as I sat drinking the instant coffee, trying not to obsess over awkward classroom moments, I recalled Frank. He came to mind like he was a distant relative, an uncle who I had visited for a time as a child, but then no more. Could it be possible that Frank was still on display? So little else on campus had changed, and surely it would not be easy or necessary to dispose of a taxidermy bear. I decided that, to mark the end of the semester, I'd go in search of him after my final class.

Although I remembered well the figure of Frank inside his glass case, I didn't recall in which building he resided, and could find no directions to help me locate him. Looking at the campus map, which showed a realm divided into arts and sciences like two hemispheres of a brain, I figured Frank would most likely be in the Biological Sciences Museum. This was at the back of the Biology building, a dark brick hulk with small, recessed windows. Inside the halls of the Biological Sciences Department I moved with the soft steps of an intruder, although there was no one around to intercept me. I passed through a corridor lined with offices, where each door had the name of a professor on it and newspaper cartoons stuck around them, curling at the edges, giving clues to the apparently stressed or easygoing inhabitants of each room.

I pushed through the door that marked the entry to the museum, and into its red ambience. Windowless, with low headroom and murmuring lights, it was like being inside an underground bunker where the memory of animal life on earth was preserved after a catastrophe. I was surrounded by all manner of animals but it was soon obvious that a Kodiak bear was not among them. I walked slowly past the embryos in jars and articulated skeletons, my gaze sliding over a turtle shell and through the open jawbones of a crocodile hatchling, as if my doing so was a spell that could make Frank appear. Then I stopped at the table with the visitors' book on it and wrote in my name, sitting for a while afterwards watching the lungfish in the tank opposite and reading the titles of the hardbound PhD theses stacked on a nearby shelf. They were on biological topics so specific I barely understood them, and I was reassured by their obscurity. My own tendency towards noticing the minute and the obscure seemed validated by the attention these authors had paid to their highly specialised subjects.

In the year that followed I often visited the museum. At first it was to check if Frank had reappeared, but then I came to enjoy the clandestine atmosphere, the company of the preserved animals and the slow movements of the lungfish in their tank. They were ancient animals, the information alongside them explained, living fossils that evolved more than 100 million years ago, and a link between fish and air-breathing animals such as humans. They dwelled at the bottom of their tank, grey and unstirring, as if they too were waiting, biding their time.

As I sat across from the lungfish I tried again to reanimate the fairytale that had been stored in my memory. Its moments were as discrete as the perspex bubbles on the museum wall in which the owls perched in frozen postures on scraps of bark. In one we picked up the weekly watch delivery from the newsagency, in another we stood beside Frank, in another we were back home, opening the envelope of watches and examining the contents. My memory had no further clues about how these moments fit together and my grandfather was no longer alive to give his side of the story.

The lungfish twitched their fins and I sat as still as if I too had become an exhibit. I let the story trail off, turned my mind to other thoughts. My grandfather had died when I was young and aimless, so he never saw the shape my life would take, nor found out that he had in part been right. I became a teacher, yes, but I had also found my vocation as a writer. My grandfather's advice to pay attention to my thoughtful nature had led me to it, as it gave me the courage to be no one but myself. But so did the music I'd listened to as a teenager that he had believed would lead me astray. Subcultures also gave me license to shape my life the way I wanted to, fuelled by the energies of dissatisfaction with the status quo. I wished that I could write like certain songs made me feel, how they could distil something pure from the mess of experience. When I wrote I went in search of that power.

Turning from the lungfish I looked over to the opposite end of the museum room. Beside a cabinet of shells and sea sponges was a door that led out to the white light of a corridor beyond, where further glass cases of specimens were on display. Deciding to see where the corridor led, I pushed through this unfamiliar exit. The hallway had a chemical solvent smell that reminded me of high school science classes. As I passed by the laboratories I could see groups of students in white coats, their attention funnelled into their microscopes.

Watching them clustering around the benches, intent on their tasks, I became a teenager again. I was back in a high school science laboratory, a Joy Division song running through my head, a band t-shirt hidden under my uniform, as I examined a slide of red blood cells under a microscope. The teacher described them as being round and concave, like butter menthol lozenges. There were trillions of them in our bodies, she said. I realised I could think of myself as a collection as much as an entity. Biological life was made up of levels within levels of detail, contained within me and all around. As much as I was able to notice, there was always more that remained invisible.

Time was moving backwards. By the end of the corridor I was a child again. For there was Frank. He stood inside his glass case, where he must have been all through the times I'd visited the museum in the last year. If only I'd known my error: I had been so close, only a corridor away. I felt almost shy encountering him again, like he was a suitor I'd left waiting for decades, and had returned to find him faithfully present, paws outstretched.

On the wall opposite Frank was an information panel that revealed his origins. In 1978 a Kodiak bear had died at Taronga Zoo and was given to the university to be prepared as a taxidermy specimen. The bear's skin was preserved, a wood and foam form made to mimic his shape, and his head molded from a plaster cast. Photographs recorded the process, a series of images by turns weird, gruesome and humorous, of the bear skin stretched out, then of the bulging foam-covered form that resembled a snowman.

The bear was named after the professor who had founded the School of Biological Sciences, but his name also suggested that he was something of a Frankenstein's monster, a combination of organic and artificial parts. Frank was made of wood, foam and plaster, glass eyes, adhesive, and the skin of a bear. He was made of the labour of the scientists and technicians who assembled him, made of the Alaskan wilderness where Kodiak bears live, made of his years in zoos that led him to this strange afterlife.

Unlike the experience of returning to a childhood playground to find everything much smaller, Frank was as imposing as ever, with the grim set of his mouth, his powerful stance, and his expanse of thick pale-brown fur. I went up to the cabinet and put my hand on the glass, watching for a twitch of recognition from inside, as impossible as such a response had always been.

The Fly

Trick Fly
29¢
MADE IN HONG KONG
NO. 7140

The Fly

The fly fidgets, bumping up against the windowpane. As much as I try to ignore its buzz the sound cuts into my attention. I turn to the window, which frames a view of an oak tree, a living photograph of pale green leaves. The fly jolts across it, seduced by the light, frustrated by the solid transparency of the glass. The sound of the fly opens up time. The buzz of its wings drills into my memory, the parts where the slightest, most incidental moments are stored.

As I watch the fly hover at the glass, a moment from the past echoes. It is the late 1990s and I'm sitting on a narrow balcony, the roar of the nearby highway prickling the air around me, as I read a slim blue book of Emily Dickinson's poetry. I am drawn to the same poem every time, 'I heard a fly buzz – when I died –'. Its strangeness moves me and I read it like a secret, a communication from a ghost, a reminder that life is momentary, is perpetual.

The next year, on an afternoon when the air smells of flowers and mushrooms and damp heat, I walk to the bookstore where Elizabeth Jolley is speaking. At the back of the room I sip water from a wineglass, watching people in the audience progressively shoo away a fly as it works its way around the room. I listen to Jolley's soft, clever voice. When she asks *How many of you are writing?* I don't dare raise my hand. The fly has alighted on it, as if I've been chosen.

The year after that I am sitting at a bus stop with my notebook open on my lap. The hot weather makes me notice things more acutely.

I'm writing a list of the objects on the pavement in front of me – a purple artificial rose, a broken cassette cover, a recipe ripped out of a magazine, a fly approaching a puddle of melted ice cream – when someone sits down beside me. It's a friend with whom I exchange letters but rarely see in person. He leans in close and says *Don't write too seriously*.

Then the next year, I'm walking over the square of earth where the house I lived in as a teenager has been recently demolished. It had been a brick house, plain and small, with kitchen benches of bright yellow laminate. Already, though, it is difficult to clearly remember its details. I stand where my room had once been, listening to the sound of Saturday-morning lawnmowers whining like flies. Like the vacant lot I am waiting, an attentive, empty vessel.

Then a year after that I'm backstage at a music festival, sitting on a plastic folding chair outside one of the bands' trailers. I can see them inside huddled over a plate of drugs. The table behind them is covered in ravaged food: strips of celery, broken breadsticks and squashed cheeses over which flies are creeping. Soon the band emerge, eyes blank, holding celery sticks. One by one they throw them towards the partition that separates their backstage area from those in the next tier of stardom, calling out *Morrissey, this is for you*.

The next year, at the acupuncture clinic, the practitioner flicks a pink-tipped needle into the skin under my belly button. There's a fly zigzagging over the window and I watch it to distract myself from my fear of the needle's sting. On the other side of the curtain another acupuncturist explains to his patient that he's about to put a needle in the point for the liver, which is also the point for anger. I hear a yelp and then a man shouting *Take it out!* The fly buzzes with renewed energy, absorbing the man's rage.

Acupuncture doesn't help me much, for the next year I'm stuck back down in the underside of life. A fly, its body the same dark iridescent green as my fingernail polish, crawls over the pub table. No one moves to shoo it away. This crowd I'm spending my time with wake up late and drink all afternoon. When I feel a pull at my scalp I see that the man beside me is biting my hair, his teeth sunk into the end of my long plait. I reach over to reclaim it as if taking a toy from a baby.

The following year I'm in the back garden of the house I have just moved into, watching the planes low overhead, coming in to land. Under the flight path, this close to the airport, the rent remains cheap. A United Airlines jet sends shivers through the aluminium skeleton of my chair, the roar of its engines filling my ears as it passes over. Then quiet. Perched on the towel hanging on the washing line, a fly turns in jerky movements like it is connected to puppet strings. Lizards dart across the fence, and ants surge in procession over the bricks.

The next year I'm out walking, on a long afternoon drift. Inside the ruin of the factory that once made tennis equipment, shreds of insulation hang down from the ceiling and the empty rooms have graffiti thick on the walls. Everything left behind has been broken. I sidestep a pile of smashed light bulbs and boxes of water-stained paper, then come to a sign for the laboratory. The entrance to it is choked by asthma weed and the buzz of flies comes from within. Fear bites me so sharply that I stop short and turn to check that no one is behind me.

The year after that I'm in an underground bar, listening to the performer on the stage. It is Kristin Hersh, who sings as if she's in a trance. Her songs are ghost stories, and I believe them, for I know that inside beauty, horror often lurks. A new song starts. I watch the image of the fly that is tattooed on the neck of the man beside me move in time with his pulse, in time with the music, in time with my own heart.

The next year I'm teaching in a classroom with an odd, parallelogram shape. Perhaps it is this skewed alignment that produces the weird mood that hangs over the students. One of them, who is particularly free in sharing her insecurities, says *I don't have ideas, I just can't come up with them,* staring at me like this is a challenge. Before I can respond another student, who hasn't said a word nor taken off his sunglasses all semester, goes to the window with the rolled-up course reader, and swats the fly that has been shuddering up and down the pane. *I guess,* the first student continues, *I just don't know why this class even exists.*

Then the year after that I've moved house again and am unpacking boxes. The boxes once held eggs or cakes or oranges, but now they contain crockery wrapped in newspaper. As I unwrap the plates I read snippets of last month's news. On one sheet is a crossword and I pause at the clue *flies partied, buzzing around,* waiting for the words to unlock to reveal the answer. But I stare and stare and just can't solve it.

The next year Simon and I approach the address where the dinner party is to be held. We're nervous because the house is larger and grander than we had expected it to be. Inside, though, the walls have water-stains, and it smells of dust and cupboards, and there's a fly in the pot of soup that is the main and only course. No one eats much anyway. We drink wine from water glasses and the loud guests get louder as the quiet ones retreat. I haven't said a word for half an hour. Through the dirty, speckled glass of the window, the full moon watches us.

The year after that I fail the test to get my driver's license, making nervous mistakes in my banal journey around the suburbs with the assessor. At home afterwards I cry as if I might never stop. Later, when I go for a walk, I wear sunglasses to hide my puffy eyes. At the bakery, the school student who works the afternoons is standing in the entrance, holding a yellow plastic tennis racquet. She swats at the air, at the tiny flies that are hovering around the door, determined to dispel them. She begrudgingly pauses to let me pass.

The next year I am at the cliff above the ocean in Coogee, standing with a group of strangers. We are all watching dolphins in the middle of the bay, eyes fixed on the disturbance of water where their fins are visible above the surface. A woman walks up to me saying *where, where* as she brushes away a fly, which comes to buzz at my upper lip and prevents me from replying. Before I can direct her gaze she cries out and grasps my hand tightly, her grip slim and hot and unfamiliar.

Then the year after that there are fires in the mountains and I listen to the reports of them on the radio. They announce the litany of road closures and the number of hectares burnt. The acrid air tastes of alarm and when I shut the kitchen window against the smoke I notice the flies trapped in the spiderweb in the corner of the frame. Behind them I see the sky is yellow with haze and the sun droops towards the horizon, smeared down the pane in a sickly red streak.

The following year I am sitting on the lawn behind the office where I spend my work days, watching a fly walk across the page in front of me, rubbing its front legs together as if the text is making it itchy. Underneath it are the words *a force in things which one had overlooked*. The words make me itchy too, for I don't like to overlook things, but already my eyes have lifted up from the page. I'm distracted by the prickle of the sun on my arms as it warms the chill of office air-conditioning from my skin, by the twitch of the blades of grass as ants move along beneath them, by the row of clouds like a string of commas.

The year after, watching the traffic before stepping out onto the zebra crossing, I see that the crash will happen before it does. Then it comes: a wrench of metal, headlights bursting in a pop of glass and plastic. A man gets out from his smashed car to yell at the negligent driver. A crowd gathers to watch but I don't join them. The accident makes me want to hide and I retreat into the back lane, where flies hover over the bins, expired appliances are piled up, and the fences are painted with warnings.

The year after this I am catching a taxi home from the hospice where Helen is in the final days of her life. Maybe I have seen her for the last time. As I left the room I had to trust she could hear my goodbye in the deep place to which she had retreated. The taxi's radio is set to a jazz station, and every time the traffic lights stop us the driver takes out a pocket notebook and writes in it. A fly is battering at the back window just behind my head, and I am blank as an automaton.

Then the next year I'm sitting in a sliver of shade underneath an oleander tree at the edge of a municipal rose garden. It's the exact middle of the week. The first hot day of the year. The phrase *concrete and roses* comes into my head and a fly zips past to underline the words in my thoughts. No one looks to be around but there's a sense of things happening just out of sight. The more I concentrate, the closer I can get to them.

The year after I'm standing in the doorway of a hotel-room bathroom, watching Steph as she takes out a plastic fly from a packet. She turns to ask me, *One fly or three?* The hotel hush that encloses us is absolute as I consider her question. We might as well be in a bubble, floating fifteen stories up over Tokyo. We had travelled from opposite sides of the world to be here together. *One*, I say, and she daubs eyelash glue on the shaved side of her head, waits a moment, then affixes the fly as if it has alighted there of its own accord.

The following year I'm walking through the concrete corridor between the multi-storey car park and the back of the television station building, on the path out from Central station. Sometimes the city folds me into it, other times it pushes me away. Today I'm on the cusp, like a fly walking on the rim of a glass. On the corner of the building is an electronic banner, a zipper of red text that broadcasts the news headlines. A warning moves across the screen: a 'heatpulse' is due in the coming days. I am part of the crowd walking towards the hot, parched future.

The window shudders in its frame as I pull it up. A moment later the fly finds the opening and soars out and away. For a brief moment it is a speck against the trees. Then it is gone.

The Sinking Horse

The Sinking Horse

They were only a short way into the journey, but now the horse was sinking into the mud and no amount of urging would convince it to move forward. As much as the boy pulled on the reins and cried out, imploring the horse not to give in to despair, it made no difference. The boy had hoped his amulet would give them both protection from the miasmic sadness of the swamp, a mood so infectious that it drained travellers of all hope. But his horse was sinking quickly, the mud now up to its neck. Just before it disappeared into the mire the boy screamed out one final cry. Then the scene faded to black as if we, too, had followed the horse down.

It's not real, my mother reassured me, it's just a movie. The horse didn't actually sink, it was lowered down through a trapdoor and released perfectly unharmed, taken back to its stable, given carrots. Adults used this method of reasoning to explain any potentially distressing movie scene. Films were made of magic tricks and make-believe, fake blood and prosthetic monsters, and on screen anything could exist without actually having happened.

Despite these consolations the sinking horse from *The NeverEnding Story* lodged in my imagination. I knew that my sympathies were meant to reside with Atreyu, the young warrior sent on a quest to save the world of Fantasia from a creeping void known as the Nothing. When he cried out his horse's name – Artax – I knew I should suffer his scream as if it were ripped from my own throat. The tale of Atreyu's journey is told inside the overarching story of its being read by a lonely, unpopular boy who hides from his bullying classmates inside a second-hand bookstore. Here the boy, Bastian, is drawn to a grand tome titled *The Neverending*

Story. He becomes Atreyu as he reads, as I become both of them by following their intertwined stories. Except I wasn't Atreyu, nor Bastian. I was the horse.

The sinking horse was an expression of the private feeling, soft and low, that soaked through me like so much swamp mud. It had been with me for as long as I could remember, as integral and connected to my being as my hands were to my arms. Sometimes it rose to engulf me but mostly it was just present, a low, constant hum in the background. I heard it like it was another melody, existing in counterpoint to the surface tune of life.

Almost as soon as I became aware I was this way I realised this was an undesirable quality. I was an introvert, a quiet observer with a morbid streak, drawn to the grisliest of fairytales. This combination set me low on the classroom hierarchy. Here I dwelled like a crab under a rock, along with the others relegated to social exclusion due to their personality or appearance or difference. My one day of kindergarten popularity came when a group of alpha girls took interest in me as if I were a pet. They grasped hold of my two long plaits, crying out 'giddy up horsey' as they trotted me around the schoolyard. It was a silly, benign game, but it made me seethe with despair, wishing I could escape the restraints of my identity. Perhaps it would be preferable to be a horse among horses than a human among humans. Horses behaved like horses, humans could be all types of monster.

Whatever had caused me to be so introspective must have been predestined, epigenetic, for I couldn't remember a time when I'd been otherwise. Personality seemed to be a lottery in which some were successful in winning appealing traits, and others were not. Observing the most popular of my peers I envied the ease with which they were accepted by others but had little longing to be like them. Despite its weight I often experienced sadness as a comfort. It surrounded me like a cloak. Sometimes it sparkled at the edges, felt transcendent, as if through melancholy I could come closer to understanding the underlying forces that shaped the world around me. I was drawn to anything that took me elsewhere, the private realm of my thoughts, or the worlds within books.

The film of *The Neverending Story* was based on the novel *Die unendliche Geschichte* by Michael Ende. An English translation of it had been published the year before the film's release. After seeing the film I started on the book, doggedly underlining all the words I didn't understand. The meaning of 'hexagonal', 'contrivances' and 'representing' were unclear to me, but I understood enough to realise that the scene with the sinking horse was different in the novel. There was a tone of solemn acceptance rather than of anguish, and a mood of restraint. Instead of Atreyu's pained monologue in the film, in the book the boy and the horse speak quietly to each other. Atreyu tries to convince Artax he will not let him drown, but the horse is resigned to its fate. As the waters close over him Artax asks Atreyu not to watch any longer, so as not to see the moment when he disappears. Atreyu nods and turns away.

The film heightened the anguish, showing Atreyu's drawn-out scream and his wide eyes as he watches Artax slip away. It was in part the changes to this scene that caused Ende to denounce the film as kitsch and plastic, a more commercial, melodramatic story than the one he had written. His novel had portrayed good and evil and the role of the hero in a more equivocal fashion, a quiet voice rather than a scream.

At the time of my reading *The Neverending Story* we lived on the rural outskirts of the city where the land had been divided into lots of five acres, big enough for residents to operate small farms. Most properties had a few horses or cows grazing in the paddocks. Our neighbours had two horses: Bing, brown like an acorn, and Mary Lou, grey as a cloud. I would watch them from our side of the fence, wishing they were mine instead of the plastic My Little Ponies that were the only horses I had a claim to. These toys had a sweet, synthetic smell and came with a name, a backstory, and a comb for their thick, shiny hair. I brushed their hair as I was intended to but gave them new stories that cast them as my favourite literary characters: orphans like Mary Lennox in the *Secret Garden*, or the virtuous but doomed Beth in *Little Women*. My sister and I would line them up on their sides, pretending they were in hospital. A few years earlier I'd had pneumonia, and so we dutifully transposed this illness onto the ponies, who languished from the effects of pony-monia, from which they would either recover or succumb.

The real horses knew none of the imaginings that the small human watching them from the other side of the fence believed it was her particular lot to dwell upon. Bing and Mary Lou would toss their heads, nicker at each other, kick up their legs, go running. In the rain they'd retreat to the brick structure that, for a time, they shared with Blip, a brown and white calf. The horses would rarely come to the fence but Blip often would and I'd touch his soft nose, feel his sweet breath on my arms. Then I noticed Blip had gone, and when the neighbour cheerfully reported him to be good eating, I cried at the heartlessness of this betrayal.

Sadness could come as much from outside as from within. In *The Neverending Story* there are two forces of despair that threaten Fantasia. The horse sinking in the swamp represents individual loss of hope. The obliterating storm of the Nothing is its exterior, collective equivalent. This malevolence sought to destroy all life, replacing it with a vacant, lightless vacuum. The two worked together, feeding off each other, forces of entropy leading towards oblivion.

In the novel Ende had intended the Nothing to be an existential metaphor but I understood it more literally, as environmental destruction. This kind of devastation was in news reports which detailed the obliteration of rainforests and the effects of toxic waste. The Nothing was in the map which showed the radiation cloud extending out from Chernobyl, and in the films that imagined the aftermath of nuclear war. The Nothing was closer to home too, in the dead wallabies by the side of the road, the land cleared for new housing developments, and the trash landscape of the municipal tip. The tip's disorder and excess was horrifying and fascinating. There was just so much garbage. At school we learnt that the polystyrene cups and burger packets that we threw away now would outlive us many times over. That there was a hole in the ozone layer that was growing and spreading. That everything from powerlines to food colouring would cause cancer. I carried with me the ominous suspicion that life as I knew it would soon be ending.

One way to live with sadness was to turn away from people, watch the horses, walk in the long grass of the fallow paddocks behind the house. Another was to attempt invisibility. At school I spoke the bare minimum, did my work obediently, and wore my hair in a single plait in the hope its potential would be ignored. My sole friend, Joyce, was similarly unpopular. We had been ostracised for our social awkwardness, but unlike me Joyce had an excess, rather than a lack, of confidence. Having me as an underling gave her some consolation, and I was a willing acolyte, imagining her to be a witch and me her apprentice.

At lunchtime we'd forgo the skipping games and groups in which we would be unwelcome, and retreat to a courtyard of round, smooth pebbles at the edge of the schoolyard. *Some of these rocks are poisonous*, Joyce said. *Touch one and you will disappear*. We then took turns in picking them up. I'd close my eyes and select a pebble at random, nervous, excited, expecting a sting as its cold weight sunk into my hand. When I opened my eyes to find myself still there – the courtyard's ivy-covered walls, Joyce's wispy hair and messy uniform, the sound of the other kids shrieking from the playground – it was always with a measure of disappointment.

This urge to disappear, to pick up the poison rock or sink like the horse, increased as I grew older. As a teenager it intensified to the point that sometimes I was sure my heart would stop from the weight of feeling impending adult life seemed to entail. In these years I was barely visible above the swamp mud but I balanced at the point of sinking, never quite slipping under. Persistence won out. The exact nature of my quest I could only know by continuing it. I came to realise that the same porous part of my nature which brought me low could be a source of power. It shaped me into an observer, a chronicler, a questioner of appearances.

This observer is an adult now, many decades on from *The Neverending Story*, sitting at a table in a cafe, looking through a book of fortunes called *The Secret Language of Birthdays*. The book is in a ragged, much-consulted state, the jacket covered in a sticky, protective plastic. I flip through to the date of my birthday. It is described as the 'day of enthusiastic belief', and the symbol accompanying it is a fish with a human face. It is the kind of illustration that might have decorated the ocean on a medieval map, the body unremarkable, a regular fish with scales and fins, but appended with a smiling, chubby-cheeked face, like that of a benevolent monk. It grins at me as I read the description of my character.

I'd been expecting the usual astrological mismatch, the description of my personality according to my Aries birth date that most often describes my exact opposite. Such descriptions congratulate me for being a high energy leader with a strong competitive spirit who enjoys physical activity. In the Chinese zodiac I am a Horse, and despite my fondness for horses, the character of the astrological Horse hinges similarly around extroversion. This book had a different prescription. It explained how the energy and enthusiasm granted to a person born on this day is often curtailed. If this person is unhappy in childhood, 'they will carry a certain lifelong sadness with them'. I nod at the page, accepting this pronouncement.

The forces from *The Neverending Story* continue to pull at me, the swamp of sadness as a loss of hope and the Nothing as environmental destruction. In Ende's novel these forces can be countered by magic, which activates the powers of one's dreams and aspirations, but in the real world there is no such fix. Life brings sadness and hope in varying, shifting measure.

The Nothing is in ecocide, in extinction lists, in climate projections. It is the blackened ground after catastrophic fires, it is the bleached coral reefs, or the grey, lifeless expanses of e-waste dumping grounds. It arises in mundane ways, too. In the crisp air-conditioned vault of a supermarket, pre-Halloween, I stare down at a life-sized plastic skeleton laid across a display of packaged candy. Its bony hands are stretched out from its black shroud as it reaches up from a plastic grave of treat-size Milky Bar multi-packs. Around the skeleton people shop obediently, pushing trolleys laden with groceries, reading the nutritional information printed on packets of frozen meals. I extend my hand to touch the skeleton's plastic claw, but then think better of it, imagining that like the poison pebble it might cause me to vanish, which is no longer such a desirable fate. Over the course of my adult life I have lost the urge to disappear. I cling to life, its joys and its sorrows, and move towards continuation and connection. The signs for this appear equally as often in my everyday life as their Nothing counterparts do.

On some days a man and a horse pass by my house on their journey down the hill towards the river. The man rides a bicycle beside the horse, a black-and-white pony which trots alongside as he holds the rope connected to its bridle. They move at a fast clip, so quickly that to see them is perennially a surprise, for they are gone and away in a blink. At first sight they are an unlikely pair, for this is not a part of the city where people keep horses. Here cats stare out from apartment windows at the forbidden exterior, and dogs wait out the day, eager for someone to arrive home from work and take them on their evening walk.

The first time I saw the man and the horse I was walking home, the last bus of the night roaring away from the stop, deeper into the suburbs behind me. The houses were quiet, lights off. There was no moon and this gave the streetlights an unusual intensity, spotlights on the dark, glistening stage of the street. The scene had all the hallmarks of a dream. Silhouetted ahead of me was a person walking a large dog, although the shape of the dog was not quite right, too wide, its gait more upright. It looked more like a horse, as impossible as that seemed. Then in a blink the two figures were gone, turned off into a side street so that I was sure I had imagined them. But the next time I saw them it was in the daylight, and I knew I had not been dreaming.

Ever since then the man and the pony have been a regular presence in my days. When I hear the clop of the horse's hooves against the road and the man's voice encouraging it onwards, I rush out to see if I can spot them. There they go. Quickly around the corner, moving fast towards the river, continuing on their quest.

The Word of a Snail

The Word of a Snail

Not a day goes by without new visitors, one or two and often more, to the cemetery beside the two churches, high on the hill in Heptonstall. The visitors are easy to identify, their movements uncertain compared to the locals, who move with a slow gait, following their dogs along the familiar path. The visitors pause at the entrance to the first church which has long been in ruins. Skeletal archways extend out beneath the empty tower, from which the doleful coo of doves echoes out. Around it headstones have been laid flat to pave the ground, so underfoot are fragments of inscriptions:

lamented by

free from sorrow

be always ready to depart

The voices of these memorial messages are softer than whispers, worn down by time. Visitors soon realise this part of the churchyard is much too old for the grave they are looking for. The inscriptions are from the eighteenth century, part of a different story to the one they have come in search of. They move onwards, past the second, rebuilt church and towards the newer graveyard in the field beyond.

Here the grass grows thickly and the sky is wide above. Some visitors have been instructed which row to choose, others must search, but even so it is not difficult to find Sylvia Plath's grave. Interrupting the grass paths between the rows of headstones there is a section worn down to earth by footsteps. This leads to a grave with fresh flowers and clusters of devotional objects, left by Plath's admirers.

This lonely place, far from those that sustained Plath's life and work, seems an unlikely location for her grave. This area of Yorkshire had been her husband Ted Hughes' childhood home and they had considered moving here, although she had struggled to imagine living in such a desolate place. One night in 1959 they had sat together in a pub in Hebden Bridge, the town in the valley below, and Sylvia had cried at the prospect of a life amid the gloomy valleys and windy moors.

The light is pale and weak in the cemetery, a walled yard in which the town's past residents are remembered by neat, humble memorials. Plath's grave is no grander than any other. If it wasn't for the tributes and the well-worn path there would be little to distinguish it. Within the border of stones marking the boundaries of the plot there are necklaces and pennies, a pumpkin, a selenite crystal sharpened to a point, a vase of withered yellow flowers, an ornamental lantern. Among the borage with its blue flowers, pens are speared into the soil as if they have grown there too, sprouting up like dandelions. Slipped in between the pens, inside the lantern, wedged underneath the pumpkin, are notes left by the visitors, folded into squares, weighed down by stones.

A woman kneels next to Plath's grave. She wears a red vest decorated with embroidery and a gold brooch glows over her heart. On one hand she wears a ring with a jade stone of a deep, watery green. She is not there alone. Her teenage self hovers like a ghost, absorbing the voice of *The Bell Jar* as if it were oxygen. A later teenage self, ill and bedridden for years on end, is there too, reading through Plath biographies and letters as if they might contain a remedy. Another self, the one who sat on a jetty reading 'Mushrooms' to a new love, joins them too. As a gift from all of them she takes a stone from her pocket. It is a flat, grey river pebble she has brought across the world for this purpose and she adds it to the others on top of the headstone, placing it between a shiny piece of haematite and a brown rock in the shape of a knuckle. She tries to keep her thoughts eloquent, as if someone is listening to them, although she knows they would be much the same as the gratitude and esteem of other visitors.

The first note she picks up from the tangle of objects left on the grave is written on pink paper with a jagged edge where it has been ripped out of a spiral notebook. In the top margin are words written in careful script, as if by someone unused to writing by hand: *Sylvia, know that your words live on, even though you are gone.* Interrupting *even though* is a string of irregular, squarish holes with curled edges, the work of snails. All of the notes are patterned this way, she notices, reaching for a crumpled ball of paper among the stems of borage. The snails have turned it almost to lace. She stretches it out carefully, reading *rocks* and *weeping* and *slept* and *rising* between the curls of snail-eaten paper.

As the other visitors have done, she leaves her own note to Sylvia. She rips a page from her journal and holds her pen over the lines, considering how to transcribe her thoughts that tremble at the point of becoming words. Eventually, she writes,

Somewhere in the back of my eye is a tiny version of you, bright as a pinhead, helping me to see.

Her favourite image from *The Bell Jar* is of the little white Alp that Esther imagines would appear in the back of her eye once she had travelled to Europe and seen the Swiss Alps in person. It was a reminder that nothing need be forgotten. Folding the paper into four, the woman places it at the base of the headstone, nestling it in among the stems. She pushes the pen into the earth beside it and it sinks into the damp soil. She listens to the wind in the trees and the doves calling, feeling that Sylvia is long gone from here, despite the notes and pens and stones and tributes that are left there to communicate with her spirit.

That night, after the sun sets and the dew has settled on the grass, the snails emerge. They slide out from the crevices where they have sheltered from the daylight, inside cracks in rocks or clamped onto the cool undersides of leaves, close to the soil. The snails move smoothly, slowly, leaving silver behind them as they edge towards the folded page. The paper is soft and fresh, wilting in the damp of night. The first snail to reach it nibbles at *Somewhere*, its microscopic teeth rasping at the paper, leaving a ragged edge.

The cemetery snails have digested many yous, many Sylvias. Nightly they greet the fresh pieces of correspondence, her story as narrated by her acolytes: that she died too soon; that her legacy endures; that she had the ability to hone, out of her own life, something elemental and essential that her readers continue to feel in their bones. The snails eat away at the tributes and the confessions and the homages that try to emulate something of Plath's chill, tender tone. They consume her words, transcribed by many hands.

The snail moves on across the page, through *bright* and *eye*, towards the far edge. As the snail edits my note I am down in the valley, in a guest room inside a house in Hebden Bridge. I sit cross-legged on top of the floral-patterned counterpane with my laptop in front of me. My vest hangs on the back of a chair, the gold brooch rests on a floral coaster on the bedside table. The jade ring remains on my finger, too precious to take off and risk losing. My grandfather had made it, polishing and setting the stone, and I wear it to keep him with me.

Hebden Bridge is the town where, in the 1950s, Plath had sat crying in the pub, and the town where, almost half a century before that, my grandfather had been born. When he lived there it had been a mill town, the stone buildings blackened by soot, the river freezing over in winter. Heptonstall, on the hill, was a windy place, he said, with bitter weather. His stories persist in my memory, as do the tears that would come to his eyes when he spoke of these places. Hebden Bridge had been cold and grim and lives there were shaped by toil. But the crags on the hilltops and the folds of the valleys and the winding river were forever a part of him. For him to speak of them brought about such an excess of emotion that I imagined his tears were the water of that river.

Much of my living has been done vicariously. Books contain my supplementary life, accompanied by my secondary family, made up of the writers who have guided me. My imagined Aunt Sylvia could write a phrase as sharp as a cut. She guided me through my languid teenage years, in which I read *The Bell Jar* so many times that I carried the scenes and places from the novel as if they were my own memories. I was Esther Greenwood in her cornflower bathrobe, standing on the rooftop of a New York hotel, throwing away her expensive city clothes piece by piece, so they were picked up by the wind and carried away into the night. I was Esther as she travelled home on the train with a grey suitcase containing two dozen unripe avocadoes. I was her again, sitting in the breezeway beside her house, at the typewriter, waiting for something to happen. Later, when I became a writer, I realised how much of writing was made up of just this: sitting at a desk, waiting for something to happen.

On the laptop screen I was following a different story of Sylvia Plath, this one written by objects. I scanned down the auction listing, noting the prices the items had sold for. They were the former possessions of Sylvia Plath and Ted Hughes, put up for sale by their daughter Frieda. The auction, Frieda wrote, was a way of telling the story of her parents' shared history. There were over a hundred lots in all, the material archive of the professional and personal lives of the two poets that had been kept by their children.

The photographs of the objects glowed with the energy of private things made public. There was an annotated manuscript of *The Bell Jar* and Plath's first-edition copy of it, inscribed with her name and the date two months before she died. There was her typewriter, a Hermes 3000, with a layer of grime and dust over its mint green casing. There was a yellow sundress, three wristwatches, and her wallet with her membership cards for the Boston Public Library and the Poetry Society of America, her signature neat on both. Her lettering was upright, the characters rounded, precisely inscribed.

The objects had sold at prices that exceeded expectations. After the auction they dispersed to collectors and devotees, who had paid the high charge for a genuine artefact, a scene Plath had foretold in 'Lady Lazarus', her poem of death and rebirth. The poem is eerily prescient as it describes the sanctified reverence surrounding her relics. Her books had been written with the hope that they would continue to be read into the future, but now her worn grey leather wallet and the tartan kilt with her name on a label inside were literary objects with their own mythologies. Plath's tartan skirt was now being worn by a London bookseller, her fishing rod leaned up against the corner of a biographer's living room, and the three delicate wristwatches once worn by her were in the possession of an American woman who was drawn to the poignancy of their stillness.

I read on through the auction listings. There was the gold dragon necklace, recognisable from the photographs I'd scrutinised in biographies, her thesaurus and her cookery book and the *Shorter Oxford Dictionary* inscribed with the names of Plath and Hughes and their children, as if it was the family Bible. Books, sketches, manuscripts, clothes: the entire debris of a life, from childhood drawings to the certificate of her Pulitzer Prize, awarded posthumously, twenty years after her death.

Dispersal, decay. I go through the auctioned objects one by one, as thoroughly as the snails move across the words of my note in the cemetery on the hill.

'The word of a snail on the plate of a leaf' is the first line of 'The Couriers', a poem from *Ariel* about suspicion and soured love. The word of a snail was not to be trusted. Snails are both soft and hard, delicate and destructive. They move slowly but are often elusive, detected by their aftermath: the holes in the envelopes in the mailbox, the plant eaten to stalks. They can be thought of as forces of stealth, symbols of decay.

In Western European illuminated manuscripts from the Middle Ages, snails frequently appear drawn in the margins, pictured in combat with knights. It isn't known exactly what the snails are meant to represent. The knights in armour brandish their swords in a show of power, but the snails are the victors. Perhaps the monks who painted these scenes were the knights who fought against the slowness of time, the inevitability of decay. The artists and scribes worked carefully, knowing they were preserving words and images for the readers who would encounter these books in the future, long after the artists themselves were gone.

The Ceramic Zoo

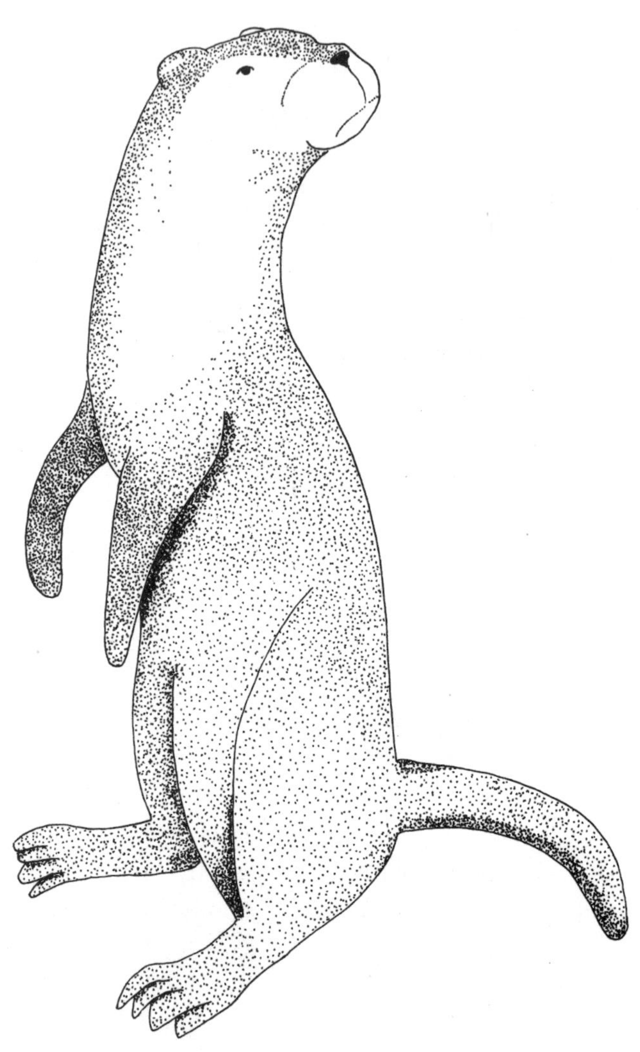

The Ceramic Zoo

Dangers came in the form of the sharp, gouging corners of benches, doors that could trap and crush a hand, or slippery bathroom tiles on which feet could lose their grip. Poisons lurked in the cabinet under the kitchen sink. Even something as small as a sewing needle could be perilous if lost in the expanse of the carpet, and it chilled me to imagine how I might kneel or step on one and have it pierce my skin.

The evidence for these lurking dangers came through particular incidents my parents repeated as warnings. Did I remember the time I had tried to climb up the shelves of a bookcase like it was a ladder? Only vaguely. Mostly I recalled the sensation of being in the dark, surrounded by books which had fallen in such a way as to protect me from the toppled shelf that I was now lying underneath, miraculously unharmed.

The house's decorative objects required a different kind of caution. I was to look but not touch, a difficult task as I found these objects fascinating. They had been there as long as I could remember, clues to how life was before I was born and the world beyond the house. Many of them had a connection to animals: two emu eggs with black pitted shells; a framed print of three horses running under a stormy sky; a piece of polished driftwood fortuitously shaped into the figure of an eagle.

In my room I kept my own collections, the kinds of toys and trinkets acquired in the course of a suburban girlhood. Among them were delicate porcelain figurines which I kept inside a glass display cabinet, arranged by type. One shelf housed tiny horses, another dogs and cats, and another a quartet of insects playing musical instruments. A grasshopper in a tuxedo played a cello, a ladybug held a pair of gold cymbals as if readying to strike them, a cricket played a violin, and a beetle a flute.

The porcelain insects were affixed to squares of cardboard that had the maker's mysterious name and origins, 'Hagen Renaker, San Dimas CA', and the instruction 'to remove – soak in water'. I didn't dare. Each cardboard label was a mooring for the small, easily breakable figure adhered to it. The figurines made me feel at once a delight at their delicacy, and anxious that they might be destroyed. Sometimes it seemed that just by looking at them I might cause them to crack.

My greatest wish was to move carefully through the world, to pose no threat to anything around me. I felt uncomfortably giant as I walked through the fields that led down into the valley behind the house. Grasshoppers sprung away, disappearing into the meadow to either side as I disturbed them from their positions. My feet flattened the grass, carving paths through it in curving, haphazard lines, like the scribbles on the trunks of the gum trees that marked the edge of the paddock. The scribbles were written by caterpillars as they chewed through the inner bark, and I sometimes imagined that I had the ability to read these markings as if they were words.

In the evenings in summer the crickets made a different music to the kind suggested by the insect figurines in the cabinet. A blanket of pulsing, chirring sound stretched out around the house, arising from the long grass. If I moved towards the edge of the sound the section closest to me would stop, like turning off a light, and I wished there was a way I could float out into the field undetected.

The house where I live now is perpetually messy, the rooms crowded, with books, papers and ornaments tightly packed on the shelves. Sometimes a section of the arrangement slips and avalanches to the floor, but I feel no danger from this. The fallen bookcase that avoided harming me in my childhood continues to enact its protective force.

Another detail that has carried over from my childhood is that many of the decorative objects around me are in the shape or form of animals. Pinned to the side of the bookshelf beside my desk is a framed embroidery of a cat, next to another of a mouse, next to another of an owl. On the shelf beside them is a shell-encrusted statue of a marlin. On the wall above the desk are postcards, a drawing of a girl chased by geese with her hat flying off behind her as she runs, beside a card with an image of Kowhai Park with its playground swings in the shape of an octopus. Concrete tentacles rise up out of the lawn, a swing hanging within each loop.

One of the bookcase shelves holds a collection of animal figurines, although not the ones I had as a child, which have long gone to a forgotten fate. Apart from a collie dog and two bluebirds that once belonged to my grandparents, most of the figurines I now live with have either been gifts or bought second-hand. They are in plentiful supply in op shops, the residue of an outmoded style of home decorating that favoured the delicate and innocuous. My collection includes long-necked cats, two matching poodles, two boxer dogs, a yellow chick, a sleeping deer, and a white rabbit. In the centre of them is a porcelain otter. It stands upright and carries a yearning expression, making me think of a dog begging beside a dinner table, rather than what I imagine a real otter's look to be, whiskery and fiendish.

Figurines reflect a charismatic, tamed version of animal life. The otter was made by Beswick, a British pottery company known for its figurines of wild, farm and storybook animals, produced for display on mantelpieces and in china cabinets. Close scrutiny of my otter's eyes reveals the irregular edges of hand-painting, the traces of a momentary touch. Paintresses in white smocks provided the paint daubs of eyes and nose that completed the otters' expressions. I know other identical otters are cherished, or ignored, or packed into boxes and forgotten, or broken and glued back together, or in antique stores, awaiting rescue.

The figurines on my shelf wear grey coats of dust, which is gritty against my hand as I pick up the otter and carry it to the kitchen. Here I rinse it under the tap so it gleams as its real counterpart might, fur slick with water, emerging from a river. The sink and the figurine are a surreal, domestic substitute. After drying it I don't return the otter to the shelf, but instead put it down beside me on the desk. In this position it is flanked by a different menagerie: a biscuit tin patterned with wrens, a row of paper clips shaped like pandas, a plastic polar bear smiling and waving from a pen lid like a friend in a crowd.

Over my lifetime my relationship to representations of animals in cute and kitsch forms has changed. It is difficult to reconcile their abundance, as mascots, toys, or decorations, with knowledge of how their real counterparts have been affected by human encroachment on their lives and habitats. It is often the species that are most vulnerable that are used for such objects. The plastic bear waves at me from a pen lid, as sea ice shrinks and I read news reports of thin, haggard polar bears roaming far from their usual habitats in search of food. Earlier in the year I had read of the influx of polar bears in Novaya Zemlya, a cold, remote archipelago, in the Arctic Ocean north of Russia. Dozens of bears had descended on the region's main town, searching its rubbish tips and streets for food, which led to a state of emergency being declared. This string of islands in the far north has seen greater threats. In 1961 the largest atomic bomb ever detonated was tested on the western coast of Novaya Zemlya. This explosion produced a fireball eight kilometres wide and its shockwave travelled around the earth three times.

The plastic polar bear on the pen lid leads me to this distant, wounded place, as the ceramic otter takes me to the rivers where otters dwell. I call up a recording of the novel *Tarka the Otter* read by David Attenborough and listen to the opening description of the meadow and river, and the otter curled up in a hollow of a fallen oak tree beside it. Attenborough's voice is as familiar as a friend's, his elongated vowels and his slight rasp like the rustle of dry grass, reminding me to pay close and careful attention to the balance of life around me.

The otter on the desk beside me keeps up its permanent, yearning gaze, unlike the quicksilver, elusive nature of a real otter. My encounters with them have been few, just a handful of glimpses in zoos here and abroad. The first time I went in search of one was on the trail of Walter Benjamin's *Berlin Childhood Around 1900*, his memoir in vignettes that describes the places and atmospheres of his early life. In one section he writes of the otter at the Berlin Zoo. He would often visit its enclosure in a neglected corner, a place where he felt able to perceive time differently, to experience past, present and future all at once. He rarely saw the otter except in glimpses when it surfaced from its activities underwater and Benjamin delighted in his insignificance to it. At home on wet days, hidden inside the house while the rain streamed down the windows, he felt a sense of accord with the otter, connected to it by the flow of water through the city.

As I sit at my desk with the Beswick otter, I am sheltering inside, but from the heat rather than the rain. It is another hot, dry summer, and most days I leave the blinds drawn over the windows to block out the heat, giving the room a confined, crepuscular mood. The ceramic otter takes me back into a cold Berlin morning, a decade earlier. I had been using Benjamin's *Berlin Childhood* in lieu of a travel guide, following his memories from a hundred years before, to see what resonances might remain. Trying on another person's memories in this way, I imagine myself into their life by replicating their journeys or looking for the places that were significant to them.

On the trail of Benjamin I crossed the city to visit Krumme Strasse in Charlottenburg, which he had described as being lined by small establishments which possessed an aura of excitement and danger. Accordingly I elevated the minor oddities of the street to a cabinet of curiosities: a shop selling fountain pens, another selling bonsais, a woman wearing all black and holding a little white dog on her lap. On her coat was pinned a circular gold brooch, a reminder of the sun that was hidden above us behind the solid winter grey of the sky. Noticing my attention, she smiled at me as if we shared a secret.

When I went to the Berlin Zoo to look for the otter it was midweek and midwinter. I was certain I would be one of the first people through the gates that morning but inside I found that many of the park benches were already occupied by the zoo's regular visitors, women who sat chatting or doing crosswords in the newspaper and drinking thermos coffee. The inexpensive yearly ticket for seniors provided them with a safe place to sit out the day, on the benches beside the llama enclosure or the rhinoceros house, a midground between the loneliness of their apartments and the bustle and unpredictability of the city streets.

The otter pool was at the back of the zoo, the northern edge alongside the canal. With Benjamin's words in mind I had the same sense of muddled time. Following the echo of his memory I sat beside the greenish water watching for the otter, but the only disturbance was the rippling on the surface from the wind. I could hear the city around me, the surge of traffic, a siren rising up, but I was separate from it, like I was swimming in another element, the air thick and cold as if it were water.

True to Benjamin's memory, I didn't see the otter. After a while I stood up and continued walking. There were more visitors now, clustering around the exhibits. A feeding display began at the seal enclosure when a man in a wetsuit entered it with a bucket of fish under his arm. He puckered his lips and the seal came up for a kiss, receiving a fish as a reward. He guided the seal through more tricks – flips, balancing a ball – until the bucket was empty. I moved to leave but the woman beside me, one of the regulars, told me to wait, he will come out with *ein andere*, another. I understood what she was saying but my own words piled up in my mind like jammed keys on a typewriter, and I couldn't assemble a reply. She went on to ask, is this your first time here? As if the following day I might join her again, come every morning to the zoo with a newspaper and a thermos, and watch the seal perform until I too knew its choreography.

Once the seal show was over I moved towards the polar bears. In front of their pool a couple were standing, arms around each other, kissing. Behind them the bears crashed and tussled, their strong legs churning the water. Again there was someone at my side speaking to me, a man this time. *Entschuldigung,* he said, the word for 'excuse me' that made me think of a sneeze. *Welcher Bär ist Knut?*

Ich weiß es nicht, I said. These words, at least, came out smoothly, for I used them often enough. There was much I did not know. In this case it was impossible for me to recognise the polar bear which had, two years earlier, been the snowy white cub that became a worldwide celebrity. Knut was a full-sized bear now, one of the four in the enclosure, all of which had the same lanky, prowling presence. The bears tumbled below as the couple kept up their kissing, and the man continued to speak to me, although I soon lost the thread of his words and understood nothing more.

After my visit to the Berlin Zoo I tucked my admission ticket into my copy of *Berlin Childhood,* where it has remained ever since. When I open the book now, on this hot day with the otter figurine on the desk beside me and my ceramic zoo on the nearby shelf, I turn to the page marked by the ticket. I read again how Benjamin listened to the rain, and with it imagined his connection to the otter, and the city alive all around him.

Wildpark

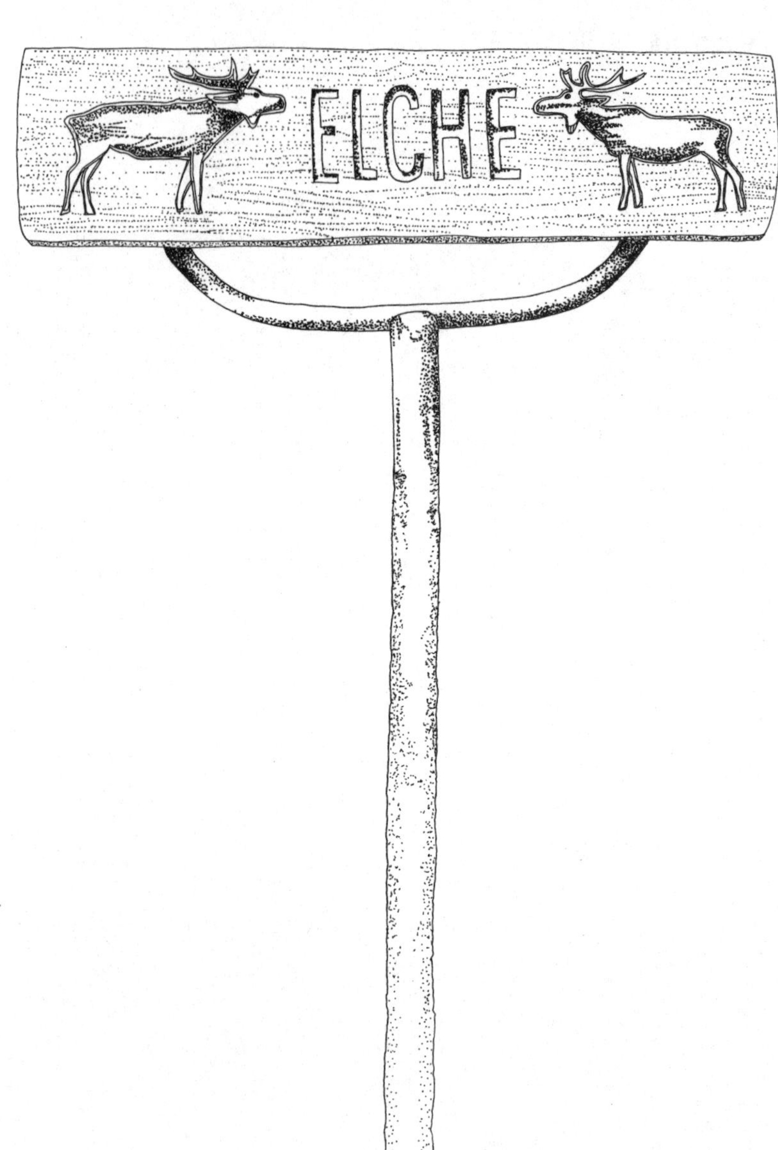
ELCHE

Wildpark

To either side of the path were bare winter trees, and as I walked along it my heavy woollen overcoat weighed my steps, slowing my progress. The coat was a kind that had long fallen out of fashion and wearing it I felt as stiff as an oven mitt. The locals wore light, puffy jackets, weatherproof and practical. The coat marked me as an outsider, but even had I been dressed more conventionally I would have been no less out of place.

From the time I had arrived in Leipzig I had been surrounded by misfortune, and in response I moved quietly, hoping to glide through without causing disturbance. When I gathered up the courage to speak, my words in German were clumsy and often misunderstood. Asking for directions to the bakery, I found myself led to the statue of Bach, and then at the bakery was given bee-sting cake instead of the bread I thought I had ordered. In this way I navigated the city, ghostly and stumbling.

The one person I had spent time with was Maja, a literature student who had remained in the city during the long winter break and was thus tasked with welcoming me, visiting from Australia. Everyone goes home for the winter, she had explained, as we sat waiting in the student lounge, beside a bookcase sagging under the weight of literary anthologies. The campus had been deserted and when we reached the building where my afternoon reading was to take place, a security guard had met us to unlock the door. The interior was dormant, the air undisturbed for many weeks. Flyers on the noticeboards recalled past events and presented the elapsed deadlines for literary prizes.

After half an hour it was clear no one was going to arrive,

so we started to plan places I could visit around the city. Maja considered this as she opened the window, then returned to the table to deftly roll a cigarette. As she smoked it, tapping the ash into a teacup, she told me that, although it wasn't the usual activity for tourists or visiting writers, I could go to see the elk at the nature reserve south of the city. I took her suggestion like it was a prescription. Her cigarette and the ash in the cup transported me back home for a moment, to the afternoons and kitchen tables at which I had sat drinking tea, watching the smoke curl up from a friend's cigarette, as we talked about everyday, easily forgotten things.

Through the open window the sky looked sullen, as if it might rain, and Maja said she had better set off for home. I farewelled her nervously, afraid I'd transferred some of my bad luck onto her. But no, I watched her unlock her bike and glide safely away across the deserted campus. Once she was out of sight I began the walk back to the guesthouse in the centre of town, where I suspected that I was the only resident. The building was undergoing renovation and from the early morning workmen hammered at the walls to either side of my room, so I felt as if I were trapped in a cave, with frantic but futile efforts to release me occurring all around.

The walk back into the city centre was punctuated by small disasters. The smash of a dropped glass rang out from inside a café. A few minutes later on Goethestrasse two bicycle riders had a slow collision, both losing balance and falling to the ground in a tangled mess of limbs and wheels. A man who, like me, had watched the accident occur from the footpath, lost hold of the piece of paper in his hand and it was swept up by the wind and away. Before the calamity reached me I quickened my pace, turning into the side street that led back to the guesthouse.

Alongside my narrow bed, across which I had spread out the map of the city, was a shelf where I'd lined up a row of foil-wrapped chocolate ladybugs and a marzipan pig in a plastic wrapper. In Germany pigs are a symbol of luck and these marzipan *Glücksschweinchen* are sold in candy shops, rotund, pink baubles with piggy snouts and cloves for eyes. I'd been intending to keep the pig as a souvenir, but I found myself tearing at the crimp that sealed the package, releasing the pig and biting into it, the taste a little like Christmas, a little like medicine.

On the map I located the Wildpark in the south of the city, a patch of green, marbled by the thin blue tributaries which trickled out from the Pleisse River. The next morning I took the tram there, a journey that passed along the corridor of flat-faced apartment buildings that make up much of Leipzig's centre. It was a grey journey for the most part, until the colourful splash of a huge neon sign, on the front of a former grocery hall, of a cartoon family at a dinner table, eating soup. At night when the sign was illuminated their arms moved, lifting the spoons to their mouths, which gave them their name, the *Löffelfamilie,* spoon-family. The building below it was graffitied and overgrown, and beside it on a plinth roosted a sculpture of a spiky, rusted dragon made of scrap metal. Leipzig had many such zones of decay where buildings kept their memories behind their grimy and broken windows.

The road crossed over the Pleisse River and I knew from my map to alight here, at the edge of the forest where there was an entrance to the Wildpark. Beside the path gardeners were sweeping up leaves, clearing the ground for the coming spring. It was too early for the trees to be in bud, but today there was an ease to the air, an indication that winter might not persist for much longer. I walked towards the map displayed at the crossroads. It was handpainted, a green square with each of the animals – deer, otter, bison, elk – drawn inside a white circle to mark their location. The elk was cross-hatched like a children's book illustration, which gave the details of the scene around me, with its bare trees and Russian log house tearoom, the mood of a folktale. I would follow a trail of crumbs deeper into the forest, a bird would alight on my shoulder, trill instructions into my ear.

Something must have gone amiss in my translation. I found myself following a man and a woman, both of them thin and grey-haired. They stopped at a fence beyond which was a churned patch of wet earth. The woman extracted a loaf of bread from her bag and she and her companion began to throw slices of it over the fence, the white squares tiling the dark mud. The bread attracted a drift of wild boar piglets, which came running up, snorting. The piglets hopped through the sticky mud, gobbling up the bread, as the couple watched with satisfaction at the scene they had created. With their nimble legs and striped backs the piglets were in contrast to the grey bulk of the sow. She lumbered up, pushing through to eat the last of the bread, skittling the piglets to either side. At this the couple laughed, as if it were a familiar sequence of events, and I realised that the pigs were characters in their shared world. A bubble of contentment enclosed them and I watched on as if I were observing a scene inside a snowdome. Shake it up and the piglets would go chasing the slices of stale bread as they tumbled inside the glass sphere.

Pigs meant luck, I reminded myself; they were a sign of good fortune. The marzipan pig I had eaten the night before was protecting me and had no doubt led me here to face its fellows. Yet I was external to the scenes going on around me, like a background figure in an oil painting, an outline of a long coat, my face a featureless smudge. Further along by the side of the path a group of schoolchildren were sitting in a cluster, filling in worksheets on which they had been tasked to draw an image of an otter, the animal whose enclosure they had assembled in front of. Their pencils outlined long shapes, decorating them with whiskers and claws and pointed ears. As they drew, the otter glared at them from the wet, trampled-down leaves at the edge of its pond, with a disgruntled expression as if it could see the distortions the children were inflicting upon it.

On the other side of the path was an aviary inside which an owl stared from orange eyes the colour of marigolds. It was a splendid bird with tufts of feathers sprouting from its ears like exclamation marks, its only movement an occasional blink. A woman with a pram stopped beside me to regard the owl, pointing it out to the swaddled baby inside the cushioned interior, as she pursed her lips into an *ooo-ooo*. The owl met the sound with another blink, impervious to the attempt to communicate in its language.

The woman with the baby was part of a mothers' group and for a while I walked among them as they pushed their prams in the direction of the elk enclosure. Amid them I was an invisible spinster aunt, although the babies could detect my presence. As I passed through the group a thin wail went up from baby after baby, until almost all were crying. When the mothers slowed to comfort their infants I walked my way free, stepping around the bulky prams with their odour of nylon and mushed biscuits.

The elk enclosure was ahead, a stretch of forest with a double fence of metal and wire defining its perimeter. The hunched shape of an elk moved slowly between the mossy trunks of the beech trees. Its heavy, chestnut-brown body was supported by thin grey legs, and it moved delicately as it continued on its solitary walk. Now I realised that the elk was the animal I knew as a moose: different continent, different name. 'Elk' had a decorated, antler sound, 'moose' was wide and soft as their blunt noses.

I stood at the fence, watching the elk amid the trees as I clutched my fingers to the wire. I listened to the cries of the babies, and the sound of the wind in the branches, carrying scraps of voices from elsewhere in the park. The sounds were from far away and as irrelevant as if I had changed into a different form where human sounds no longer carried any meaning. My feet had taken root in the soil, my body had transformed into a beech tree, my head was in the clouds.

A new sound arose, a thump and a huff of breath, as the elk approached the inner line of the fence. He nosed his soft snout along the bars and I watched his long, serious face, with prominent brow bones like a horse but wider, looser lips, which quivered in expectation. Instinctively I checked my pockets, but I had nothing to offer him, just a one cent coin, the slightest of all currency. *Nichts*, I said, but the elk continued to regard me, thinking I had something for him.

I took off my gloves and turned my empty hands palm up. As the heat dissipated from my skin I imagined my aura, lemon-yellow. The elk breathed it in with my smell, part wool, part human. We stood there separated by the fence, alone, together.

A Spider in My Cup

A Spider in My Cup

The television glow lit the room a flickering, underwater blue, although it wasn't water that surrounded me. It was night, which enclosed the house, the suburb, the city, all together underneath its cloak. The sound on the television was turned down low, so as not to wake my mother, asleep after a day at work, or my sister, young enough to be afraid of the dark. The house was hushed from their sleep and I moved with careful, exaggerated movements when I crept out from my room. Newly a teenager, I had become nocturnal, like the possums that rustled and thumped in the roof, or the cats by the fence that hissed and squalled like evil spirits.

The night opened another world to me. Graveyard-shift radio shows played angular songs interspersed with snatches of dialogue, or sounds like the glitching of anonymous machines, as if broadcast by ghosts. On weekend nights the opening credits of the music video program *Rage* flicked like the closing of an eyelid, ushering me into transmissions from a collective subconscious. Sitting close to the screen I bathed in its light and absorbed its images, the volume minimal so the songs only scratched at my ears.

Some were stranger than others. The stranger the better. I craved weirdness, the subversion of ordinary life and order. My childhood had given me ample time to register social expectations, to know the ideal was to be extroverted and physically confident and to wear at least a veneer of happiness. I was so much the opposite that I couldn't even pretend to be otherwise. In late-night music videos I hoped to catch glimpses of others of my kind.

At midnight I came quietly out of my room like a spider emerging from a curled leaf. Tonight there was a special feature on The Cure and I had no desire to sleep. The Cure's world was one of eyeliner and tangled hair and reality shirked in favour of dreams. Their songs turned on a hinge of melancholy and bliss and I entered them like I read novels, stepping into something simultaneously imaginary and real. The surreal scenarios of their video clips, featuring palm trees in the snow, a wardrobe falling off a cliff, or a house teeming with kittens, heightened this sense of reality turned askew.

The hours ticked past as their songs advanced through the 1980s. By three a.m. they were at the end of the decade, almost up to the present. Filling the screen was the red-lipsticked face of Robert Smith, his head sunk into a pillow, chest rising and falling in a way that made me immediately conscious of my own breathing. This song 'Lullaby' told the story of being pursued and eaten by a spider, which in the video is also played by Smith, dressed as an evil version of himself. His lyrics whisper and groan as the music creeps forward, itself a spider, a thick, bulbous body in the bass notes, the violin melody smooth like a skein of web.

Despite the spooky attic set and the ghostly figures, the video should not have been particularly frightening. It was cartoon menace, the malevolent spider-Smith scraping at the grimy window with long fingernails, as the regular Smith in his striped pyjamas lay paralysed with fear, tucked in under blankets in a narrow cast-iron bed. Surely it was meant to be as much camp as eerie, but I heard the song as a warning.

It was about a nightmare, or about drugs, according to the music press, but that night I understood it to be a song about destiny. The inexorable movements of the predatory spider were like a ticking clock, measuring out the duration of my life. At the end of the song Smith slipped into the spider's furry maw, disappearing completely. On screen the image faded to black. I reached out towards the light zap of the screen's static, and followed him in.

The spider was adulthood, was life, was death. With every advance across its web I was carried forward in time. The spider moved me slowly onwards through the illness and fatigue that consumed my teenage years. At fourteen something changed within me, and I was so tired that I could barely wake up, let alone get out of bed. My head was in a fog, my limbs ached like they were ready to snap. There was nothing I wanted more than sleep. After months had gone by without improvement I was diagnosed with chronic fatigue syndrome, a newly defined condition which was only vaguely understood and tenuously accepted. Doctors had little clue to its cause, how to treat it, or how long it would persist. You might never recover from it, one of the specialists said, the truth is we just don't know. The treatment was patience, waiting, and sleeping my days away.

For a while my life happened mostly in my dreams. Sometimes I'd lie in bed only half asleep but unable to move, hearing the sounds from elsewhere in the house, voices and movements both magnified and remote. I slept twenty hours a day but it was never enough. When awake I'd lie in bed listening to music, my eyes tracing a line between the desk and the wall. In this space lived a daddy-long-legs spider, so slight inside its tangle of web that it might have emanated from the dust. Sometimes a movement disturbed it and it would spin in circles, so fast it turned into a blur. But mostly, like me, it remained at rest, waiting for something to change.

Spiders were my companions. I'd never been afraid of their erratic movements and scuttling legginess. The way they took up residence in the house's hiding places, its seams and joins, cracks and corners, reminded me how I too was hidden away, my body restricted to the bed. My eyes roamed over the room's textures, snagging on its details. From the ceiling hung cobwebs in a dusty mesh that, periodically, my mother would come in and sweep away with a long-handled broom reserved specifically for this purpose. Before too long, though, spiders would spin their webs anew.

The radio was my companion too, the community stations late at night with their niche programming. My favourite was the goth show, *Sacrament*, which played gentle grey songs or booming grandiose ones that spun delight out of the sad and strange, creepy and nocturnal. Music for spiders, for bats and black cats. In between the songs the host, with her sweet high voice that rang out like a bell, called me further into her world.

By the end of my teenage years I had recovered enough to half-function in the everyday world, although the everyday world was not where I wished to spend my time. I wanted to live a nocturnal life; I went in search of the goths. Maybe the approaching end of the century had coaxed them out of their hiding places, for every week there was at least one club night where I could linger at the edges of the room and watch the fully-fledged goths, who moved with the confidence of ravens. The country op-shop visits I had made with my friend Natasha had given us the requisite attire of black velvet and lace, now we just needed courage. At Shrine we drank spirits that glowed blue under the UV lights and watched the dancefloor from a corner table. Amid the smoke-machine fog, the goths moved in graceful, spidery arcs around each other, content to be tangled in the same web.

Spiders respond to vibrations to register the movements and disturbances around them. This was how my unfolding life felt.

I sensed my way, without a plan for how my life would progress. By my early twenties I had left goth behind, as a time capsule in which Natasha and I remained side by side in our long black dresses. I had the habit of staying awake until two or three a.m., using the quiet of the night to write out the details of the day just passed. I wasn't writing only to remember. Like the spider, which weaves a web from its own threads, I was writing myself into being.

I lived at the edge of the city, in a narrow top-floor apartment where the floorboards groaned underfoot and many decades of residents had left their traces. The kitchen doorframe had layers of pencil markings recording the heights of the kids who once must have lived there. I wondered about them as I sat on the step beside it, sipping the coffee that was strong but yet never quite woke me up properly. Who had Jarrah grown up to be, who was Moholy? They too had lived in these rooms, looked out these windows, sat on this step.

There were plenty of cobwebs but I had no tall broom to sweep them away. I watched the webs sway from the ceiling in the breeze that came from the open window, which brought the heavy roar of the highway traffic and people's conversations from the alleyway outside. Often these were banal but I would listen regardless, to the wreckage of other people's lives, couples breaking up, or one friend remonstrating with another. I lay in bed listening, trapping the scraps of their conversations, writing lines from them in my notebook. *I can't stop it rolling away,* or, *Dario this is bigger than you and me.* I devoted myself to recording as much as I could. Every detail stuck in my web.

Perec's Cat

ISBN 0-00-271464-7
9780002714648
GEORGES PEREC
Life
A User's Manual

Perec's Cat

In the author photograph that fills the back cover of *Life: A User's Manual* Georges Perec has a black cat perched on his shoulder. The cat looks out over his cloud of unruly hair, her light eyes round and watchful. Her glossy tail stripes the front of Perec's pale, cable-knit cardigan, as he levels an amiable gaze towards his readers.

Perec had a succession of pet cats, all of which went by the name Duchat. The Duchats had an essential quality by which one could transform into another. This was echoed in their name, which means something like 'McCat', or more literally, 'of the cat': they needed no additional identity besides their feline nature.

These two complementary spirits accompany the readers who hold a copy of *Life: A User's Manual*, who see Perec's homely knitwear, and his unruly cloud of hair like uncontained ideas. Some might notice the shadows under his eyes, and how his face is both tired and lively. The night before the photograph was taken he had been up late, perhaps, at a party, or setting a crossword, or writing a description of the objects on his desk, or thinking over the events of *Life: A User's Manual*. The novel traverses the lives of the residents of a Parisian apartment building through a series of short chapters that move from character to character, apartment to apartment. He plotted the novel using a grid of one hundred squares, with the story progressing in a zigzag path across it, a 'Knight's Tour' of an irregular chessboard, covering all squares but one. This one untraversed space made the system forever incomplete, like life, which never goes exactly to plan.

Perec's writing was shaped by the constraints he placed upon it. Words could be playthings, like strings are to kittens. In the preamble to *Life: A User's Manual* he wrote of puzzles, and how every move the puzzler makes, the puzzle-maker has made before. The puzzle-maker guides the puzzler as the author guides the reader. The trick is to make it seem otherwise.

—

Duchat flicks her tail and moves across to Perec's opposite shoulder, distracted by a disturbance above. A flock of birds, flying past in a flurry of grey wings. It could have been the pigeons Perec had watched at Place Saint-Sulpice some years before. For three days he had sat in the square making notes on everything around him, as an experiment in describing details which are not usually noticed, because they are mundane or functional or fleeting. Within this list buses and cars and people go by and pigeons group and disperse, moving as a mass, like a collective consciousness. On his final day of observation, one of the last notes he makes is that the pigeons all fly away at the same time. They lift from the square and are fixed on the page in that errant motion.

As the camera shutter clicks, Perec follows Duchat's gaze up towards the sky, before she jumps down. He feels the release of her weight, watches her sidle away and disappear from view. He turns back to the camera but the photographer knows the defining image has already been captured. They move back inside the apartment and Duchat climbs up to the roof, where she sits, looking across the grey slate tiles and terracotta chimneys. The city is below her. She sets out, moving over its maze as lightly as she walked over Perec's shoulders.

The roofs sit over the apartment buildings like hats on heads. Underneath them the lives of their residents continue. *Life:*

A User's Manual is set in such a building, at the fictional address of 11 Rue Simon-Crubellier in the 17th arrondissement of Paris. At the end of the novel, before the appendices, there is a diagram of the apartments which acts as a map. A tall rectangle is divided into ten horizontal sections and then further vertically into individual apartments, inside which the names of the inhabitants are printed. The top two rows are crowded with names across the smaller squares that indicate the attic rooms that were originally maid's quarters.

Near the beginning of the novel a white cat is described as being shared between the residents of these attic apartments. It appears in one of the early chapters, snoozing on an orange bedspread in the room of the elderly butler who attends the wealthy Englishman Bartlebooth, who lives in one of the large apartments on the third floor below. As the novel progresses and the apartment building is brought to life, the white cat remains dozing inside this sentence, content to sleep through it all.

On the rooftops Duchat moves softly but deliberately. She winds around chimneys and passes by attic windows. The scenes occurring inside them, so vital to the participants, are of little interest to her. The residents of these small apartments sit alone with their morning coffees, read correspondence, or pause in moments of reverie, surrounded by the cluttered or meagre evidence of their lives. To these people, if they notice Duchat at all, she is similarly anonymous. A black cat, her shape a silhouette as if cut out from the rooftop scene behind her.

When Duchat passes the window behind which the white cat Pangur slumbers, lying with her paws tucked underneath like the fold of an envelope, the two cats sense each other. Pangur lifts her head and opens her eyes, one blue, one yellow. The cats pause, staring as if a mirror has tricked them. One has the quiet interior as her domain, the other the rooftops beyond.

They blink, ascertaining their territories are safe from each other, then Duchat moves on to further roofs and Pangur sweeps a look around the room in which she sleeps. A narrow wardrobe bulges with clothes, the door hanging open with the patterned arms of polyester dresses protruding. A roll-top desk is piled with papers, its nooks and drawers full, the only vacant space a recently cleared square, the size of a sheet of paper, on the desk's surface. The chair is pushed back, unoccupied. The woman who usually sits there is out working her job as an attendant at the Museum of Natural History. At this moment she is explaining that a gentleman's large umbrella must be left in the cloakroom. He doesn't like it, and pauses as if he's going to refuse, then relents, watching as a label is clipped to this precious accessory.

The cat closes her eyes, gets back to dreaming. She travels back in time to her namesake, Pangur Bán, who dreamed by the side of the monk who wrote a poem in her honour, more than a thousand years before. During his time living in the abbey on Reichenau Island he inscribed the poem in his copy book, between the grammars and hymns on which he practised his hand. He wrote how he and Pangur shared a like task, as Pangur's hunting of mice was like his capturing of thoughts. The monk sits hunting words all night, while Pangur Bán waits to pounce on the mice that scuttle out from the walls.

The poem is an ode to Pangur Bán but also to the hermetic joy of working late into the night on a task which has one's heart. The outside hush encloses you as activity concentrates in your thoughts, gathering energy to pounce upon an object. Sometimes ideas might be slow in coming, but as with waiting for a mouse, if you have patience and sit quietly, one will surely appear.

This Pangur Bán is a less active muse. She spends most of her days and nights sleeping. Like the monk the woman often stays up late, writing until two or three a.m., sitting at her desk with her legs crossed, the foot of her top leg tucked behind her lower calf. She sits for so long sometimes that when she uncurls her legs she feels as if she is opening a stubborn, rusted lock.

How do I know this? Pangur is my cat, and this is my apartment. This is my desk with its papers and talismans, among them a thirteen of hearts playing card, and a printed fortune for a person born in the month of April, stating I am one of the 'leaders rather than followers in all enterprises'. I often think of this phrase as I am clipping a label to an umbrella, or smiling obligingly at the professors and students who visit the museum.

Above my desk are two framed pictures. One is an illustration of boys in red shirts and grey trousers running in an egg-and-spoon race, spoons held out in front of them with eggs balancing inside the rounds. The picture is cropped and the spoon of the boy in the lead is cut off just where the handle extends, so it is forever ambiguous whether he managed to successfully convey the egg and win the race. Sometimes I imagine that he wins, sometimes that he drops it to the path below.

The second picture is from the 1960s, a black-and-white photograph of a woman and a ginger cat. The photograph is square with a white border, of the kind taken with a Kodak Brownie. The woman lies against the arm of a sofa, with her feet tucked up, so her body forms the shape of the letter N. She has a serious look, her arms folded across her body, the set of her mouth firm. This is in contrast to the fat ginger cat slumped in the crook of her legs, eyes shut, paws dangling in blissful repose. They nestle together, Lily, my grandmother, and Ginger, the cat.

For anyone else this photograph is of a stranger, the kind of photo you might find in a box at a market, among lost or discarded family snapshots. You might pick it up and wonder what this woman is thinking, with her stern, sad expression. I do too: the photo was taken long ago enough for my grandmother to look unfamiliarly young. I recognise the shape of her face, and Ginger's feline repose, but the photograph still holds mystery.

Like Perec's Duchat, Ginger was one of a succession of cats which all shared the same name. Ginger replaced Ginger, one after the other. The tradition ended before I was born but the Gingers lived on in stories, the Ginger in the photo being remembered as the most resplendent and favoured of them all. His habits and predilections were spoken of with great affection and I was sure that his ghost sometimes returned to visit. When I lay curled up on the same couch I could sometimes sense his soft weight against my legs.

Ginger's ghosts were regular presences in my grandparents' house. My ankle would itch or a breeze would tickle up against my hand and I would imagine it to be a Ginger sidling by, moving invisibly along the threshold between past and present. Later when the house was sold the Gingers went with it and I kept this photograph close to remember them, that time, my past.

Below the framed pictures, on the desk's surface, is a yellow notebook with an illustration of a ship on the cover. The ship floats above the name Lutèce, the French name for the Roman city of

Lutetia, which was built on the land that would become Paris. This book is my journal. It is never a good idea to read the journal of someone you know, for its contents will surely displease with their banality or candour. But I am unfamiliar enough to you, and we can at least look at the last words I wrote before closing the book in the quiet, pre-dawn dark that morning: *Pangur curled up beside me, under the spell of sleep. I watch her but I can never know her completely.*

While I sit at the desk writing, Pangur sleeps. Cats have no need of diaries. The cat of the novel *I Am a Cat* by Natsume Soseki explained it thus: 'We live our diaries, and consequently have no need to keep a daily record as a means of maintaining our real characters.' Cats have different priorities, as Soseki's cat reports: 'Had I the time to keep a diary, I'd use that time to better effect; sleeping on the veranda.'

Soseki's cat was an observer, allowing the author to step to the side of the elements of human nature he wished to satirise. In the first part of the novel the cat appears as a stray kitten at the home of a teacher and his family. Initially the kitten is expelled from the house, but the teacher relents and allows it to stay. The family tolerate the cat and the cat tolerates them, becoming a cynical commentator upon the humans he lives alongside. When the teacher shuts the door of his study, ostensibly to work, the cat sees how he dozes over his books instead. The cat listens with disdain to the gloating conversations between the teacher and his friends, and decides that 'all humans are puffed up by their extreme self-satisfaction with their own brute power'. Humans are cruel but also petty: the teacher rarely records in his diaries anything but his illnesses and complaints.

Across the street from my apartment where Pangur sleeps, Duchat returns home, slipping back in through a window left open for this purpose. Underneath the window are piles of books. When Perec wrote of his methods for sorting books he described the many locations they can be housed in addition to shelves: between two windows, in the recess created by a blocked-off doorway, or on the steps of a library stool. Wherever they are placed it is a difficult task to order them. This lack of order can, however, produce useful results, serendipitous discoveries during the search among the shelves and stacks. Attempting to instil order on books, or life, or anything, we waver between the illusion of completion and the abyss of the ungraspable.

Duchat pauses for a moment on top of the stack of books, licking one front paw with her rough tongue. It tastes of soot, of roof tiles, of the scenes she has passed over on her journey above the city. Now she rests on the purple and yellow cover of a paperback copy of Sei Shonagon's *Notes de chevet*. Perec is hoping to write his own version of Shonagon's pillow book, adapting its categories and lists and free-floating associations to the present-day. So far he has extracted from it her comments on fashion, dividing them into sections, 'outerwear', 'skirts with long trains' and so on. In the same manner he would like to tell the stories of the objects on his desk: the blotter, the bud-vase, the teapot shaped like a cat.

The teapot has been moved from the desk since Perec included it in this list. It is now one of the non-book objects in the bookcase facing the desk. It has a pinched expression on its ceramic face, as if it is obligated, but unwilling, to pour tea from the upraised paw which makes up the pot's spout. This unwillingness continues into action, as when the pot is tipped the cat's head that is the lid wobbles, threatening to detach.

Only Duchat animates the placid, midday atmosphere of the apartment, as she sits atop the pile of books. Perec had felt the pull of the city when he walked downstairs to farewell the photographer. Soon afterwards he himself set out, walking along Rue Linne towards the Jardin des Plantes. At the street corner he passed by the Cuvier Fountain, a curved trough above which a sculpted goddess sits amid a medley of stone animals. To one side of the folds of fabric that drape her lower body is an owl with a puffed, proud chest; to the other the stern face of a lion stares out with blank white eyes. Below the clamshell on which the trio are positioned is a cluster of marine and amphibious beasts. Here a stone crocodile performs an impossible movement, turning its head to look back behind it, as if seeking something forgotten.

When I pass by this fountain on my way to work at the museum I only have eyes for the crocodile. Its pose of retrospection seems a torture and I long to have the power to untwist it so it faces forwards, even though I likely would not survive this manoeuvre. In the moment of me freeing it the crocodile would sink in its teeth. I have similar thoughts at the museum, imagining the horde of animal skeletons contained within the Gallery of Comparative Anatomy coming to life and trampling me in their rush to escape.

The animals continue to await their day of revenge. It won't be today they wake. The only visitors this morning, apart from the man with the umbrella, were a couple whose wonder for the exhibits was equal to their wonder for each other. On my rounds I saw them standing in front of the glass case of taxidermy leopards. I caught the man's look as the woman gathered up her hair: he gazed at her as if she contained all the world. It was a look not meant to be observed, and I moved quietly away, my steps soft as a moth.

In the afternoon I walk back home for lunch, anticipating the quiet of my room and the bread and salted cucumbers that await me there. I move swiftly through the Jardin des Plantes, towards the iron gates that lead on to the fountain and then the cafés and photocopy shops of Rue Linne. As I rush out of the garden gates I stop abruptly to avoid colliding with another walker, a man with a cloud of curly hair and a wiry beard, wearing a cable-knit cardigan. He stops too and my apology tumbles out: I'm sorry, I say, I'm going home to see my cat. He grins and gestures me onwards, says, *Go, go, hurry*. With his absolution, I again quicken my step.

Lassie Come Home

Lassie Come Home

Against the back wall was a shelter made from tarpaulins and the rough wood of a packing crate, inside which the dog slept on a bed of faded blankets. Inside the house I would stand close against the glass of my bedroom window so my line of vision was just acute enough that I could see him curled up asleep. Often in sleep his paws scuffled and twitched and his lips trembled. He went chasing in his dreams and I tried to imagine them, the smell of dry grass and a rabbit dashing through a field, a swiftness that my body ached to follow.

Sometimes we dreamed in tandem. My bed was on the other side of the wall from where Billy slept on his blankets. When I lay awake in the middle of the night and the door to my fears swung open, knowing he was close by kept the cold, grey hands of panic from wrapping around me. Sudden sounds had him up in a jolt. I would hear the jangle of the tags on his collar as he stood to attention and knew he would protect me.

We'd only recently moved away from my grandparents' house, where my mother, sister and I had spent the awkward years of my parents' separation. Now we lived in a plain, brick house with a frangipani tree out the front like a gnarled hand. The memory of how the rooms had looked at the property inspection lingered, how it had been filled with another family's things, in the places where now our furniture and objects were only just beginning to settle. We too were taking time to settle, into a different version of a family, just my mother, sister and me, and Billy.

Billy rarely came inside, only during the worst of storms. When rain flooded the garden we'd move his blankets into the laundry, setting up a wooden gate between it and the slippery cork-tile kitchen floor against which his claws would skid. The gate I recognised from photographs of me as a baby, in which I grasped the same thin pine slats that now marked out Billy's temporary share of the house. He'd lie on the blankets, eyes following our movements in the kitchen, waiting out the rain.

The back garden was a wide square of lawn with an old shed that had grimy windows and a musty smell of dead snails. In the first few months my mother planted some young trees that we talked about as if they were additional members of our family. The *Cupressus Coneybearii* was a wide, shaggy cypress, the *Ginkgo biloba* had leaves like tiny fans, and the *Camellia sasanqua* bloomed with sweet-smelling white flowers with yellow interiors, like papery fried eggs. On top of the cinder-block fence, the boys who lived next door would sometimes crawl along, peering into our garden as if it were enemy territory. By all rights we should have been friends, but I could never think of anything to say to them, an embarrassing but not unusual situation for me.

Mostly the brothers stayed in their garden playing fighting games, pretending to be soldiers. I heard their yelps over the wall as they traded insults: *arsewipe, pisswacker.* By contrast, my sister and I were as obedient as dolls. Fiona would be inside, practising the piano, or standing on the grass with a tennis racquet, hitting a ball against the back wall of the house, bouncing it up against the bricks. I'd sit on the slight incline at the back of the garden, thinking over the same persistent questions. How was it that places and people could change around me, and yet I could remain myself, still essentially the same? This question, along with wondering if there were a way other people could listen to my thoughts, preoccupied me.

Inside the house there were distractions from such concerns. My bedroom had books and trinkets, the kitchen had the biscuit tin with shortbreads and Iced VoVos inside. I'd go out to the living room to lie on the couch or the floor to read or watch television, avoiding looking over into the corner where the mahogany upright piano waited for my infrequent practising. Fiona had the ear for music, I just wanted to dream.

It was school holidays, the afternoon hours stretching out long and hot. Standing close to my bedroom window I looked outside to see Billy asleep. He was curled up so tightly I didn't want to go outside and disturb him, so I moved towards the living room and the thin whine of the television in the corner. We had a habit of switching it on as background noise, so it would often be playing to no one, just the unoccupied room. The screen beamed in an alternate reality, busy with stories from the outside world and other imaginations.

On screen was a scene of a farmhouse amid fields. White sky, grey fields, a boy calling to a collie dog: an old black-and-white episode of *Lassie*. Daytime television lagged decades behind the present, persistent in remembering family-friendly American series from the 1950s and 60s with their neat, prescribed realities. Each program had a quirk which disrupted the order of everyday life. *Mister Ed* starred a wisecracking talking horse, the Addams Family were happy living in perverse ghoulishness, and *I Dream of Jeannie* suggested that domestic strife could be remedied by a blink or a nose wiggle. These television worlds played out either in black-and-white or in saturated colours that made my own surroundings appear faded by comparison. The viewer was guided through them with music that swelled and receded according to the level of tension, the jokes flagged by peals of canned laughter.

This episode of *Lassie* was from the early 1960s series, its storyline that Lassie was the pet dog of Timmy Martin, a boy with dimpled cheeks and a habit of getting himself into minor calamities on and around the family farm. Beside Timmy, polite with his neat blonde hair and his tucked-in shirt, Lassie appeared lavish. Her coat was soft and windswept and her long nose a precision sensory instrument, guiding her towards trouble and distress.

I sat down in front of the television, cross-legged on the carpet, to watch the story unfold. Lassie stood barking at the farm's gate, refusing to move until Timmy followed her. She then led him out to the thicket where there was an eagle caught in a coyote trap. The eagle's wings stretched out as it tried to fly away, but it was hobbled by the metal clamp on its feathered leg. As it struggled it cried out with a rasping shriek.

The scene was fiction, but on the screen it was happening at such close proximity that I felt it in my soul. The trapped bird made me nervous, guilty that I belonged to the species that caused its suffering. I knew too that far worse things were occurring for real at that very minute, and unlike in *Lassie* they would not be redeemed. On screen it was a different matter. Timmy crouched down on his belly, crawling forward. The scene cut to the eagle cocking its head, attentive to something below it – Timmy undoing the trap – before the metal jaws released with a snap, and the eagle flew free.

The character of Lassie came from *Lassie Come-Home,* a novel published in 1940. It was based on the author Eric Knight's childhood memories of growing up in Yorkshire and stories of dogs which had found their way back after being separated from their original homes. In *Lassie Come-Home* an impoverished family sell their son's collie to a wealthy duke who takes the dog to his estate in Scotland. Lassie's longing for the boy is so intense that she escapes and journeys hundreds of miles to return to him. Knight was never to know of his character's success, as he died in a plane crash before the release of the film adaptation that went on to make Lassie famous.

The television version of Lassie knew humans better than they knew themselves, and could repair the mistakes that had come about through their folly. However far the situation went into danger she could be trusted to bring it back. Along with the generations of children who watched *Lassie* I imagined something of her spirit existed in our own family dog. Perhaps Billy also had an ability to understand the logic of the human world, what we consider just and good and worth protecting. Billy hadn't ever saved me from a burning house or a freezing river, but in any time of upset or difficulty I would go out to the garden and he'd come up and sit beside me, pressing up close, a warm anchor to the here and now.

Of the dogs of my life Billy is the one that I knew and loved best. He arrived as a puppy when I was a child, and lived to the age of thirteen, by which time I was in my early twenties. He spent most of his last years asleep on the front porch. He was slow and stiff by then, his muzzle white against his brown fur. In the years after he died I still expected to see him there, alert to the sound of the gate latch to which, no matter how frail he became, he would always lift his head.

The only dog that lives with me now is a Lassie figurine, a keepsake from my grandparents' house, where it had resided on a hallway window-ledge alongside two ceramic bluebirds. Approaching from the outside I would see their indistinct shapes behind the frosted glass of the window. Then, after stepping over the threshold, I saw them properly, sharply defined against the glass. The house had the same effect of bringing me into focus, providing a deep comfort from its stability. I had chosen Lassie and the bluebirds when it came time to pack up the house and select what domestic mementoes I would keep. Along with the figurines I kept the kitchen clock, an aluminium tea canister, and two small prints in circular frames of ballerinas on a stage and of a castle, objects to sharpen my memories around.

The Lassie figurine is of a mass-produced kind, with a ridge down its back from the mould in which it was cast. Brown paint highlights the furrows in the porcelain that suggest a long, flowing coat. It has a repair to a broken front leg, a stripe of glue showing where it was sealed back into place. Over time the glue has turned yellow and transparent like amber. The repair to the complicated three-piece break had no doubt been made by my grandfather. I can imagine him performing the operation with the broken pieces laid out in one of the Petri dishes he used for watch repair, setting up the twin tubes of epoxy glue employed for such tasks. When he prepared the epoxy he enjoyed showing me how you had to mix the two substances together to activate the adhesive. He was right in suspecting that I, like him, had an interest in this kind of alchemy. I would look on as he mixed the glues together with a toothpick, releasing the scorched smell of dental fillings that came with the chemical reaction.

I keep Lassie and the two bluebirds in a shelf in my bedroom, and my eyes often go to them. With Lassie is my memory of the hallway floorboards' creak, my grandmother's slow step, and the clocks all chiming together on the hour. I envisage it almost as if it is real, but even in the most vivid of my mental images, there are shadows and elisions. Sometimes, when I come up against a shadow, or feel the edges of what I remember and what I imagine, I wish I could step through memory, be truly inside that time and place again as if it is the present.

—

The lights are switched off and the glow from the streetlights edges the curtains, which have been drawn across against the night. The corners of the furniture have a faintly perceptible gleam, in such subtle contrast to the space around them that they could be rocks or the backs of sleeping cows, rather than a couch, sideboard and chairs. The room has a dormant atmosphere, its air thick against my skin, as if I am standing in the shadows behind a closed eyelid.

The heavy plastic torch weighs down my pocket. Wearing my overcoat I'm a silhouette, sealed into one solid shape, but in the low light my edges feel as indeterminate as those of the lounge chair beside me. We could even be made of the same stuff, my presence no more significant than a footstool or a cabinet.

With the torch clicked on, its weak moon of light scans the room, retrieves the details that have been lost in the dark. A print of ballerinas, fluffy as cygnets, hangs in the corner in a circular plastic frame, above another print of the same size and shape, of a castle amid a mountainous landscape. The torchlight moves along the couch cushions, each of their covers a different texture and pattern. I had once imagined them to have different personalities. The burgundy satin cushion was a man with a thin moustache who performed magic tricks; the textured floral one was a woman who had long wavy hair and played a harp.

Every object had this kind of double life. On the surface each was one thing – a cushion or a decorative print or an item of furniture – but it had an underlying character, born of its size and shape and texture, and the stories I knew, or invented, of its origins. Each one I could enter into. The room was as complicated as a city.

The torch-beam eye moves over the wide arms of the lounge chair, made of a turtle-green vinyl. Were the chair to stir I could imagine it moving with slow, paddling strokes of its wide arms. Behind it is the dining table with the brown laminex top of imitation wood, hidden underneath a sticky plastic tablecloth, the kind which adheres to elbows and hoards toast crumbs. I move the circle of light across the table. At the centre, along with twin tubes of epoxy adhesive, is the Lassie figurine. It lies on its side in a glass Petri dish, with the pieces of its broken leg laid out carefully beside it, awaiting its impending repair.

Animal Chronicle II

Animal Chronicle II

In the city I was safe from the fires that burned along the east coast all summer, but the incessant days of heat and wind and smoke made them ever present. They were a taste in my mouth, a sting in my eyes. The fires burned through millions of hectares, razing the forests, and with every day of fire the scale of animal suffering and death escalated.

On the hottest days the fires burned catastrophically fast. One early January day the temperature reached the high forties. The air pressed at me, full and greedy. I did little but sit with my phone and refresh the newsfeed and the maps of fire activity, the spreading patches of grey overlaying the areas of green that represented the east coast forests. A cloud of smoke, dirty and thick, came over from the south where the largest of the blazes were burning. Watching it move across to obscure the sun, a heavy, saturating dread moved through me. It was akin to the feeling I'd had as a child when I thought about nuclear war, fearing the inevitable, imminent disaster and there being nothing I could do to stop it. Within my adult body I felt small and afraid.

The trapped heat inside the house was oppressive, so I spread a blanket out on the withered grass of the yard and lay out there, though it offered no respite. Every few minutes a new headline appeared on the news blog, charting the spread of the fires and reporting on the emergency responses. Then a headline came that was eerie in its directness. *It's turned to shit,* it said, as if these hastily composed words were all the reporter could manage in the face of the disaster.

Cutting into my attention came a pinging sound, like slow

hail hitting the bonnets of the parked cars. I looked up into the boughs of the fig trees that line the road. On a high branch was a white cockatoo, busy eating through the fruit, which were round and tough like green marbles. It was steadily chewing through the outer skin of the figs then dropping them down on the cars below, over and over, ping, ping, ping. I put the phone down and listened to this incessant sound, fixing the scene in my memory. The moment when the cockatoo was patiently eating the figs, as smoke came over to fill the sky, and I felt heat and fear all through me.

—

At first the estimate of animal deaths was 480 million, then one billion, then more. The numbers bulged out at me from the screen with each revision. This estimate only included the mammals, birds and reptiles: including insects, the loss would be much greater. News reports gave the details. Animals lay dead on the scorched earth as far as could be seen. Dead livestock were piled by the roadside. Shorelines were thick with drifts of dead birds which had been swept out to sea with the clouds from the firestorm. These were not isolated horrors; they were scenes that repeated across the vast scale of the firegrounds.

A year before I'd been staying on Yuin country, three hours south of the city, an area in which fires were now burning. When I was there the pace of the day was set by the animals that came past, kangaroos in the morning, wombats at night. There had been a group of ravens that regularly appeared outside the house, stalking over the lawn with their determined waddling gait, or sitting up on the powerlines. One day I caught sight of one of them on the grass, head cocked, considering something in front of it with its icy white eyes. It stayed concentrating like this for a few minutes and then hopped away. I went out and saw the object of its attention was a long, blue-black feather: one of its own, perhaps left for me, or at least I liked to think of it that way.

Every afternoon I walked into the forest and climbed a hill that was studded by outcrops of wide, grey rocks, patterned with skirts of lichen. I had chosen a particular rock with a flat top and a rise at the back which cradled my head. Lying on it I looked up at the slim, tall trunks of the eucalypt trees, absorbing the energy of my surroundings. The lichen in its starry spread, my eardrums vibrating with the shrill of the cicadas, the Wonga pigeon calling out its car-alarm bleat, and the rock warm and firm under my back.

—

The smoke settled on the city, obscuring the horizon, clinging to the valleys. On the smokiest days there was an eerie stillness. I heard no birds and saw little movement outside. Only the occasional person walked past, moving quickly to be inside and away from the polluted air. Social media documented scenes tagged as the 'new normal': photographs of the sun, red and weak behind a haze of smoke, or selfies in which people's faces were half-obscured by their breathing masks.

It didn't feel normal, this stillness and suppression, and for there to be days on which ash came drifting down from the sky. Standing at the bus stop I watched it descend around me. When I put out my hand a tiny frail leaf, burnt to a grey skeleton, landed on my palm, the ghost of something once green and alive. I touched it and it crumbled away into dust.

When I boarded the bus no one could see that behind my mask my lips were thin and anxious, and behind my sunglasses there were tears in my eyes. Although the bus was crowded there was a sombre mood, edged with fear. People sat with their eyes closed, or watched their phones, or looked outside at the white air. I followed fear along, imagining a dystopian world of only cities and burning forests, where animals were extinct or rarely seen, only to be remembered through objects. The woman beside me had a phone case in the shape of a frog, which she clutched to her chest. Another wore a spotted shirt patterned with smiling lions. The intended cheer of these designs fell flat, like jokes to which no one was laughing.

—

Anwen and I organised a reading to raise money for a wildlife rescue in one of the areas worst affected by the fires. To make a poster for it I searched through my book collection for a suitable image. I hadn't deliberately set out to collect old natural history encyclopedias and children's compendiums of animals, but they were reliably found cheaply at op shops. I was drawn to their taxonomies and descriptions, while knowing there was more to animal life than could ever be contained within the covers of a book.

Among my collection is *World of Strange Animals,* by the Czech scientist V.J. Staněk, published in 1966. In one chapter the enlargements of insects, with their protuberant compound eyes and serrated mandibles, make them seem like creatures from science fiction, although it is naive of me to imagine them so. Insects have existed for many millions of years longer than humans, and the notions of science, or fiction.

One section of the book pairs photographs of animals that share a particular feature despite being otherwise different. A whiskery catfish and a cricket with long antennae both have 'sensitive projections', a porcupine is covered in long thick hair in a similar way to the robber fly, and the large eyes of both the caiman and the loris allow them to see in the dark. Other sections consider how humans might understand animals' experiences of life, and interpret the snarl of the leopard or the monkey as a warning, or an expression of fear. Primates, one caption proposes, can have expressions so familiar that 'we often feel they share our most secret thoughts'.

Turning the pages of the book I remembered that between now and the last time I had looked through it, a few months beforehand, billions of animals and insects had died. Time was cleaving this way, into before and after.

For the poster we chose a photograph of an echidna held up by a human hand. The echidna is curled into a ball, its spines radiating out, dense and sharp, a contrast to the unprotected skin of the hand that holds it. Echidnas can survive fires by digging into the ground, curling up, and entering a state of torpor, suppressing their metabolism and lowering their body temperature until the fire passes. The echidna was survival, the hand support, and the pale grey background a future sky.

—

I wake up to thunder and then hear the rain. I imagine it soaking into the parched ground, dry from months of heat and years of drought. As welcome as it is there's a melancholy to its soft sound. It was falling here in the city and falling over the firegrounds, where instead of nourishing the trees and soaking into the earth it damped down the ash and smoulder of the retreating fires.

A phrase came back to me, a description of how fire is used in

Aboriginal burning practices: *fire should move like water*. This fire trickles slowly over the land, burning only the undergrowth. In this way it clears it and allows for regeneration, as part of the practice of caring for country. The land where I had lain on the flat warm rock had been burnt in this way the year before I visited it. The lower trunks of the trees showed the marks of the fire, and the forest floor was blackened, but from it grass trees sprouted, and here and there were the purple and red blooms of orchids. The canopy above was green and untouched. This was in contrast to the arid grey images of forests after the bushfires had blazed through them, of tree trunks burnt to charcoal, spiking up like tally marks.

The rain brought relief, but also spread the destruction to the waterways. The rainwater swept the ash and debris into the rivers, suffocating fish which were now dying in their thousands. The fish floating belly-up in the shallows was a new image to add to the reel of horrors, and I felt chastened for imagining rain as an end or a reprieve.

—

'Shifting baseline syndrome' describes the adjustments that occur with each generation, who take their point of reference for ecological diversity from their youth. I might wonder why I no longer see Christmas beetles or bogong moths in plentiful numbers, as I did when I was a child, but children now would not even know to miss them.

Noticing and recording the animals around us, and how they have shaped our lives, is a way to fight against collective amnesia. If I live into old age I am now halfway through my life. In forty years' time I might retell the story of this summer. The breadth of destruction, how many animals were lost, and people's efforts to support those that survived and remained. How it was a turning point. But now, writing this, I can only imagine, with hope and fear, what it is that we are turning towards.

The Curragh

Kys ta Shiu?
QUOCUNQUE JECERIS STABIT
LAXEY WHEEL
Song of the Manx Cat
A tale of the night and a tale of the day
A tale of the cat who has gone astray
Tales of sorrow, and tales of glee
Most things have tales,
But there's no tail on me.
Ellan Vánnin

The Curragh

Looking down through the window of the plane I could see the blue expanse of the Irish Sea, ten thousand feet below. Against the surface of the water were tiny white crosses, a forest of wind turbines. Then, in the distance, was the outline of the island, familiar from maps, an irregular patchwork of green. There was the main island, the Isle of Man, and below it the Calf of Man, an offcut of land at its base with the adrift appearance of a stray postage stamp. The plane turned above the Calf to line up with the runway of the airport on the eastern side of the main island, readying to land.

For years I'd had a postcard from the Isle of Man leaning up against the windowsill in my kitchen. I'd bought the card at an antique fair, attracted to the weird scale of the enormous red waterwheel perched amid a verdant hillside. The island's symbol – a triskelion of three running legs, a shape like a truncated starfish – was cast in relief on the front of the wheel's footings. The card's prominent position in the kitchen led me to stare at it so often that the wheel started to turn in my mind, and I suspected that I might one day stand within the scene it displayed.

Other fragments from this faraway island came to join the waterwheel. In a second-hand bookstore I found a collection of Isle of Man fairytales, with a cover image of a winged merman lifting up a mermaid child from the sea, and tales about creatures with names like the Buggane and Phynnodderee. Then I came across a magazine article about Gef, an animal spirit in the form of a mongoose that, in the 1930s, was said to have taken up residence with a family who lived in a remote farmhouse on the west of the island, attracting a series of paranormal investigations. There was also the Manx cat in Virginia Woolf's *A Room of One's Own* that Mary Beton notices walking across the university lawn as she turns to the window to tap the ash from her cigarette. The Manx cat's tailless form causes a shift in her 'emotional light' by virtue of its strangeness.

My own emotional light was altered by another Isle of Man animal story. Scrolling through the news one day I stopped at a headline that announced that wallabies were 'flourishing' on the island. I imagined wallabies sweeping across farmlands, displacing the cattle and sheep, and on through the village gardens, but the explanation was this: in the 1970s a small number of wallabies escaped from a wildlife park in the north of the island, into the surrounding wetlands. The sheltered environment nurtured them and their numbers grew. Now they are regularly seen grazing amid the area of marshland known as the Ballaugh Curragh.

When considering introduced species I usually think of northern hemisphere animals imposed on the south, as colonising presences to modify, control and exploit the land. That it is regarded as a novelty when wallabies or kangaroos have broken out of zoos and estates in Europe is in line with the colonising narrative – that this should be stranger than encountering a fox or a deer in Australia might be – but I like to think of these wild wallabies as tipping the power balance back to some small degree.

A life in Australia has taught me to see expanse and distance, but on the Isle of Man the dominant feature is enclosure. The towns are small and cling to the coast. On the journey north to Ballaugh village the hedgerows bracket the road and beyond them the fields and farmland stretch out green, brightened by the yellow ripple of gorse bushes. It is spring, and despite the grey, misty afternoon, the fields glow with the season's new growth. The towns are quickly passed through, clusters of houses with white walls, grey roofs, and bay windows behind which, occasionally, a person can be seen sitting with a mug or a newspaper, looking down reading or out at the cars passing by.

The bus draws away, leaving us in front of The Raven, a pub set askew to the road, with a black feather painted on its hanging sign. We go inside and are only there a moment before a local comes over to greet us. I recognise him as the man I'd been corresponding with about the wallabies in the Ballaugh Curragh. His name is John but he introduces himself as Dog, the nickname from his childhood by which he is now best known. Our plan was to go walking together in the Curragh, in the hope of catching sight of the wallabies.

As we set out in his van he explained how he had been going out into the Curragh for fifty years now, following its return to the wild after centuries of agriculture. He'd been drawn there first for birdwatching and in that way had come to know it, registering its changes with the seasons and the years, devising pathways through the swampland. As he told this story we progressed along increasingly narrower roads until we stopped at a nature reserve on the edge of the Curragh, bordered by fields which rippled with lighter and darker shades of green. In a few months' time, Dog said, this will all be in flower with thousands of pale pink orchids.

We followed Dog, walking a few paces behind the beacon of his bright blue coat and his well-worn leather hat. The path alongside the field became a boardwalk through a marshland, with willow trees rising from islands of turf within channels of still, brown water. If we had been here a thousand years ago, Dog said, this would be a lake. As the climate became drier the lake became a swampland which was then used for farming, drained to grow hay and graze cattle. After farming ceased the land rested, returning, over decades, to become swamp again.

As we walk he stops to point out ferns and flowers, and the fungus known as 'fairy lugs'. He drops onto my palm a light, cold, curled scrap. You dry them out, he says, and give them to children, tell them to soak them in water to make them swell up, so they seem to grow into little ears. I tuck the fairy lugs into my pocket and we progress along the path, Dog identifying the ash trees growing in among the willows. In a hundred years' time, he says, this area will all be ash and sycamore trees. The ash trees will grow higher than the willows, soaking up the moisture, drying up the land.

Time slides forward as I look over at the ash tree, imagining its thirsty roots, season after season. This cycle of change will outlive us, but I see as if through a telescope, a vision in which the three of us walk through the future forest, and Dog says, Remember the first time we came here, a hundred years ago?

Ahead of us is a wooden tower amid the trees, a bird-hide that Dog had built with his brother. Inside, sitting at the observation window, a man and a woman peer out across a field, binoculars at the ready. Seeing much? Dog asks them. Not a great deal, the man says, we saw a hen harrier go over and that's about it really. His voice is flat as he continues to look through his binoculars, barely turning to acknowledge us, he is so preoccupied with his watching.

The hide smells of wood and earth as if we're all inside a tree, looking out through the trunk. A heron appears in the distance, dipping its long grey neck down, and the warblers continue to chatter, invisible among the trees. We leave the birdwatchers to their vigil and drive a short way further into the Curragh. Dog stops the van by a curve in the road from where we can enter the marshland. Ignoring the footpath ahead of us he veers off between the trees instead and we follow. Immediately we're enclosed by the damp dark green of mossy trunks, and the twisted boughs of willow trees. They lean almost vertically, the wet, lumpen skin of the bog rising up underneath, sending the trunks askew.

Amid this landscape of moss and crooked trees we proceed along a path of narrow planks, which are only just clear of the marshy ground to either side. The wet surface of the earth has a sheen, which reflects the tangle of tree branches and the white-grey sky above, as if the trees were growing up out of a mirror. The plank path is so narrow that there is little separation between us and the marsh to either side. The branches, which twist overhead, hold us in like a basket.

Hearing Dog talk of his years of walking through the Curragh I consider the place I might regard as my equivalent, the mangrove-lined river in Sydney beside which I go walking. It is called the Cooks River, the most colonial of names, but it is also known as Goolay'yari, 'pelican' in Dharawal, in connection to a Dreaming story in which a man becomes a pelican, his footprint visible as a small island near the mouth of the river. The river runs through what is now an urban area and has been much changed in conjunction with this development, but the water continues to follow its ancient trajectory, mangroves lining its banks. The muddy surface is punctured by the short stubs of tree roots, bristling up around the mangrove trunks. These roots break the surface in search of oxygen, and so I imagine the whole stretch of mangroves slowly inhaling and exhaling a long humid breath. When I go walking there, we breathe side by side.

Here at the Curragh, the marshy ground has a different kind of energy, tighter, inkier, colder, an oil painting rather than a watercolour. I don't have the same sense of breathing but this place has its own rhythms, and if I were to walk here often, I would come to know them. I'm thinking this when, far out amid the thicket, I see the movement of a grey shape against the trees. I stop and fix my gaze on the motion and the neat face of a wallaby comes into view, framed between branches. It stares over at us from the grassy bank where it has been grazing, activities suspended while it assesses how much to be wary of us. We have paused too, to peer through the tangle of trees, as Dog tells us about the first time he saw one, shaking his head as if, despite countless sightings since, the first provided a lifetime's supply of surprise.

The wallaby lowers her head, satisfied we pose no threat. Then I see that further back behind her there's another, as the three dark spots of its eyes and nose, crowned by pointed ears, become visible amid the puzzle of tangled branches. It is a familiar thing to see them despite the inky, still landscape. I know the pace of their movements, how their postures go between upright alertness and leaning down to graze. As we continue Dog points out the prints of their long toes in the mud, leading onto the pathways they have made through the swamp. The trails look deceptively like ones we might follow until the low branches close in above, sealing them off from human passage.

We come to a crossroads where a wooden marker is etched with an arrow and the outline of a bird with a long thin beak. A curlew, Dog says, though they are disappearing, their numbers have dropped hugely in recent years. He mimics their call, two notes ascending. As he does so I realise that, over the time we have been out walking, the bird song has intensified, as the end of the day draws closer. An incessant sweet singing continued behind our own voices. Blackbirds, Dog says when I ask him, and he whistles in duet with them for a moment.

As we continue, turning back to begin our return journey, more wallabies become visible in the distance, through the trees. Some turn and bound away, others pause, more distracted than afraid. The Curragh, with its willows and moss and twisted branches with grey beards of lichen, is kind to them, and them to it, and there is little for them to fear. We walk on and they settle back down to grazing, and pay us no more attention.

Fly Away Bird

Fly Away Bird

On the hillside above the ocean a flock of magpies is dispersed across the lawn. They move slowly with their heads cocked, listening for stirrings beneath the surface. They can hear the earth being turned by worms, and the movements of insects in the grass. Occasionally one will stab its beak at the ground, emerging with either a worm, or a bewildered look that passes in a second before it returns to listening.

The magpies are my companions as I follow the path towards the expanse of flat rocks at the tip of the headland. Many are young birds with a skittish, curious energy, disinclined to move no matter how close I pass by them, which feels like their tacit approval of me. My ears are filled with the roar of the wind coming in off the ocean and the waves hitting the rocks, but I'm also hoping to sense something else, a suggestion of a presence, of my friend Helen, gone for two years now.

Helen had been as close to me as a sister. We met in the late 1990s, when both of us had been teenage misfits, writing in our zines about the absurdity of suburban life and the music that saved us from it. We shared tables at zine fairs, travelled to our favourite suburban op shops, went on picnics, had tea parties, dyed our hair, and established a tradition of baking together every Boxing Day, celebrating our friendship as its own version of family. I loved her strident, tender ways, and how she constructed the world around her as she wanted it to be. Cuteness was a transcendent power for her, which could unlock kindness for oneself and all living things. In her illustrations and comics her alter-ego wore a ruffled dress and boots, and was accompanied by canaries, little grumpy dogs, cakes and flowers.

She died at thirty-five, of cancer, after a year of suffering that stripped my heart. I knew the inevitability of her illness, could see how her pain intensified, but some part of me didn't want to believe it until it happened. Three a.m. The phone beside me, buzzing in the drawer. It was Lauren, Helen's wife. I knew what had happened before I answered. Yes, Helen was gone. Lauren described the moths bumping and fluttering against the lights outside the hospice, as if to accompany Helen's departing spirit. We spoke for a few minutes, then said goodbye and there was silence, the house dark, everything still apart from the ache which moved all through me. Anticipation had transformed into bitter knowledge.

One of the confounding aspects of grief is the contrast between the pain of loss, acute and interior and lonely, with the oblivious churn of life as it continues all around. After Helen died my experiences were both sharp and indistinct. Details seemed etched too clearly. The corners of things glistened, over-defined against their backgrounds, but beyond this time and space seemed mushy, a grey blur. Driving home from her funeral, past shopping centres and houses and construction sites, I perceived them as if they were obscured by fog. Details reared up in the foreground, then receded, all of them indifferent to the journey I was making.

Along with grief came a yearning to make connections between the living world and Helen's spirit. Up until now I hadn't thought I believed in any kind of afterlife. It wasn't the first time someone close to me had died, but I had never felt such a strong desire for communication between myself and the person who had gone. I turned my attention to potential messages and found that a layer could be placed over the days, in which signs were abundant. They could be regarded as communications between Helen and me, little things that would otherwise seem insignificant, or go unrecognised. They could be as minor as the unicorn pattern on the shirt of someone sitting in front of me on the bus, or a stripe of prismatic light falling in a rainbow across my wrist.

In particular I noticed magpies. In the weeks after Helen's death the same bird came every day to eat the berries from the bush outside my window. The berries were set into red, crown-like sepals, which gave them a heraldic appearance. The magpie was grey-feathered, young and clumsy. It struggled to stay upright, wings outstretched as a counterbalance as it weighed down the thin branches of the bush. Often it missed the berries in its lunges towards them, so when it did manage to eat one I felt satisfaction on its behalf. The magpie came daily. I'd hear it rustling and turn to watch it through the window, wondering if Helen had sent this companion to lighten my heart. The pragmatic part of me suppressed this idea: it was spring and the berries were ripe. The systems at play were not spiritual ones but instead the cycle of the seasons. Yet I wanted to believe.

The headland is the place I go to be with her. It holds my memories of our shadow selves, walking this same path I now walk alone. A line of banksia trees hems the edge of the grass slope that leads down towards the sharper incline of the rock ledge. We had often gone swimming here, in the pool cut into the rock platform under the cliffs. The rocks have a lunar look to them, grey and pitted, which leads me to call it the pool on the moon. I think of us floating in its watery gravity. Now when I visit I sit on the rocks, facing the ocean, sending my thoughts out into it. The sky and the water have the power to break me out into something eternal.

One morning I was sitting on a rock when one of the magpies

from the hill hopped up to me, watching with eager attention as I wrote in my notebook. His gaze followed the movement of my pen as words flowed out, *the sea is rough this morning, churning white beyond the rock platform…* The bird was close enough for me to see the hooks at the end of his claws and his powerful, grey-tipped beak, and how he inclined his head like a delicate instrument as he watched me. A black shape flew down as another magpie arrived on the rock, then another, until there were four in all, arranged like the points of a diamond. They put their heads back and started to sing, a chorus of sweet-throated melody. People walking past on the nearby path stopped to watch as the magpies sang to me, and I felt shy, enchanted, their message received.

Helen had an affinity with birds and often greeted them, whistling two descending notes through her teeth. When we were together she'd sometimes interrupt a sentence this way, having heard a bird call out nearby, as if she was conducting two conversations at once. For a time she wrote me messages about the baby magpies that came to visit her in her garden, birds she had nicknamed Doogle and MacGoogle. As I recovered from the initial wave of grief after her death, this was the Helen I tried to imagine in my mind's eye, whistling as she fed the magpies, rather than the traumatic memories from her year of illness.

During the Doogle and MacGoogle era we had exchanged magpie stories. Magpies, she wrote to me in one message, aren't magpies at all! It was true. They were named after the European bird, which is of a different species, but the British colonists had regarded them as equivalent enough. In the Eora language the names for magpies are *djarrawunang, wibung* and *marriyang*, and across the continent and language groups there are many other names, and ancestral stories of dawn and fire that connect to the magpies' song and the pattern of their black-and-white feathers.

The Australian magpie shares little with its European namesake apart from their similar colouring and inquisitive nature. The European magpie is a black bird with a stout white breast and a long, blue-tinged tail. I remember the time I first noticed one, when I visited Glasgow as a student, there to attend a literature conference. One afternoon I went walking with another visiting student in the necropolis that covers the hillside east of the city. We watched a black-and-white bird hopping over a lawn beside the stone monuments and my friend called out, 'Hello Mr Magpie, how is your lady wife today?'

When I asked if she usually talked to birds this way she turned to me with a serious expression, surprised by my ignorance: 'You must always greet a magpie if it's alone, otherwise it's bad luck,' she explained. She had greeted the lone magpie to ward off the sadness that it was said to bring. 'One for sorrow, two for joy,' she recited, and on through the numbers.

That birds can be interpreted as omens, with the ability to communicate between human and spirit worlds, is an idea that has existed across eras and cultures, and is borne out in daily encounters. Birds behave according to impulses external to humans, but their communicative habits can be readily filtered through human ways of thinking. As the magpies sang to me on the rocks above the ocean, I translated it according to my yearnings, as a message of joy: *all is well! all is well!*

The birds shuffled the notes back and forth in their throats like they were sifting them, turning them over for all they were worth. If it wasn't a direct communication from Helen, I let myself imagine that the magpies sensed that I missed her, and that they could provide company in her absence. It was true their song was more likely to mean *this is our place* and *what food do you have for us?* but perhaps these were not such different messages. They sung to goodness and the hope of plenitude.

The Eurasian magpie has a percussive call, very different to the fluting melody of the Australian bird. This chattering call is one of the factors which contributes to its reputation as a bird of ill omen. On the painted ceiling of the magpie room in Sintra Palace in Portugal they are used to represent gossip. When I visited Sintra, a town in the mountains northwest of Lisbon, I walked up the hill towards the cluster of white buildings with two conical chimneys like witches hats that I recognised as the palace. The magpie room's ceiling is divided up into triangular segments, each one containing a painting of a bird holding a rose in its claw, and in its beak a ribbon printed with the words *por bem,* for good. In the fifteenth century the king had decreed the room to be painted this way after gossip went around the court that he had been unfaithful to the queen. There are 136 birds, one for every woman in the court, their messages a warning to speak only for good. Each bird was intended to be a voice of conscience.

The rooms echoed with talk as I moved through them. Words bounced off the tiled walls, so the palace was alive with speech. Most was tourist patter, *ooh look at this* or *I wonder what* or *after this let's*, but the echo abstracted them into noise. In the magpie room the ceiling too was speaking, *por bem, por bem*, each bird confined in its triangular frame with its painted terrain and faded rose. A guide was telling her group the story of the king, each of her phrases rehearsed for clarity and economy. When the shuffle of their footsteps receded into the next room I looked up at the painted birds, and imagined setting them free, opening the sections of ceiling like they were hatches. The magpies would fly out over Sintra, over the yellow and pink houses clinging to the hillside, towards the mountains. The ribbons would trail from their beaks and they would let them go to drift down over the town, *por bem, por bem.*

My magpies sang for good with me on the Maroubra headland that day. When their song ended and they flew away I decided that I was going to accept all the signs as they appeared. What did it matter if I believed Helen spoke to me through the details of the world around me? It was a private relationship, suggesting sympathetic energies between surface details and other, unseen forces. Since that day magpies have been my surrogates for the friend I can no longer have by my side.

Sometimes the magpies seem to deliver a message, but often they are just there beside me, observing and listening to whatever passes through their domain. I watch the group move together across the grassy slope. They spread out across the lawn, all facing in the same direction, moving at a slow deliberate pace, examining every inch of it. Their territory can remain the same for decades, and those not paired up with a mate live in groups that share and defend the same area of land. I take heart in the knowledge that magpies have good memories, as part of their keen, attentive natures. This memory includes their ability to recognise human faces, and through repeated interactions, identify individuals as sympathetic or threatening.

It is wishful thinking to believe that they might remember Helen and me there, but the idea comforts me nevertheless. She and

I have been a small part of this place, part of the story of the animals and plants, wind and weather, rocks and ocean. Whenever I come here and walk out along the path that extends through the magpies' lawn I purse my lips, and whistle two descending notes in greeting.

Junk Bug

Junk Bug

It was an irregular, messy thing, small as a pinhead. It would seem to be nothing more than a tiny ball of random matter, but for the fact it was walking on thin, almost imperceptible legs. It looked to be made of dust and grit, the kind of bits and pieces that gather in corners and drift across surfaces and are chased by brooms and vacuum cleaners.

The insect's meandering gait was something like a beetle or a ladybug, but it lacked their gemstone charm. It wouldn't be considered a good omen, unless it was one that came from realising the vitality of even the smallest of things, or the power of something believed to be inert come to life.

Underneath its ragged carapace, legs as fine as filaments progressed the insect over the pitted landscape of the house brick it was traversing. It carried its burden lightly, seemingly without impediment, despite its awkward and lopsided appearance. Reaching the edge of the mortar it paused, assessing which direction to turn. It set off into the valley between the bricks and I too moved, standing up from where I had been sitting on the front step, to go back inside the house.

Messy looking bug, I typed into the search engine, producing results about bed bugs and the evils of household clutter. *Dust bug,* I tried, leading to information about dust mites and how to vanquish them. *Bug that looks like...* I typed, and a list of suggestions assembled: scorpion, lobster, dragonfly, leaf, and then *bug that looks like dirt*.

The insect I had been watching was the larval state of the lacewing, otherwise known as the 'junk bug'. As it scuttles over foliage it consumes aphids, flies and mites to gather energy for its transformation to its winged, adult state. The 'junk' on its back is made up of scraps and wisps of dirt and lichen, but mostly the husks of its victims, which comprise a gruesome shield and camouflage. Each bug carries a different, misshapen bundle, a record of the insects that have fatally crossed its path.

Junk bug, I wrote on a slip of paper, then affixed the note under a clip, on the side of a desk tray, along with an unusual thirteen of hearts playing card I'd found on the pavement; a list of items I had forgotten the context for (eyelid landscapes, green hawk, raven, pumpkin); a non-winning scratch lottery ticket with the face of a cackling witch on it; and a temporary tattoo of a heart with the word 'library' printed across it. With the identity of the junk bug noted I clicked shut the screen of lacewing search results, opened a document file, and went back to work.

My week continued as usual after this encounter. Some days felt electric, others were tedious, but all were accented by the momentary observations that everyday life brings. These details were as small and random as the junk bug, engrossing for an instant, but then rapidly scampering away. Perhaps the only change was in my increasingly vivid dreams. In one I watched the back legs of a horse – just the legs, without a body – walking in a winter landscape of snow and black tree trunks. In another I owned a little dog that could sing and speak. At first it was my pet but then it began to replace me in my regular affairs, going to work in my stead, and driving the car while I sat in the passenger seat with my head out the window, feeling the wind ruffle my hair.

One morning, as I awoke from another of these uneasy dreams, I found myself transformed into a gigantic insect. I was lying on my front and an uncharacteristic weight pressed upon me from above. When I tried to turn to see what the cause of this uncomfortable pressure was, my body, a segmented torso supported by six thin translucent legs, protested the movement. I managed, with some effort, to turn to the side so I could glimpse my reflection in the large circular mirror on the opposite wall. Where I expected to see myself I saw instead a messy bundle of miscellaneous personal papers. I recognised the colours and textures of the bundle, which were notes in my handwriting mixed in with letters, postcards and photographs. These scraps, which I had understood to be safely contained in boxes and drawers and tins and stored in a bookshelf, were now attached to my back.

What had happened? I was in my usual room, with its familiar fixtures, the lamp with the red shade beside the bed, the framed print of an owl watching from the wall, my journal lying open from where I'd been writing in it before I'd gone to sleep the previous night. I thought of sleeping longer, so that I might wake again to find myself restored, but the shock of having woken up in an unexpected form had made me restless.

As I moved to turn around, the objects on top of me rustled. I found I could, with the pair of pincers that extended out from the top of my head, reach up and back and move the things that comprised the pile. If I took them off one by one, I reasoned, it would be easy to return each thing to its rightful place. Until I was free from underneath these objects I wouldn't be able to go to my desk in the next room to start work. Already it was mid-morning and the day was running away from me. Emails would be accruing. As if to remind me of this fact I heard the forlorn trill of the message notification on my phone sound once, then again, before it fell silent.

The architecture of my carapace seemed to be that the objects were held in place by rows of flexible, curved spikes that extended out from both sides of my body. This formed a structure like a loose net within which the papers were arranged. My pincers investigated the objects and the papers slid and settled, creating more space on top. Resisting the urge to reach down and pick up the journal I had been writing in the night before and add it to those on my back, I instead pulled out a tuft of papers from the bundle, and brought it down to the floor in front of me.

Spreading them out over the carpet with the tip of a pincer, as if fanning out a deck of cards, I looked over the selection of papers. They were, as I had suspected, an assortment of the ephemera which I ordinarily kept stored away in old biscuit tins. Each tin contained a core sample of a particular era of my life but in the sheaf I'd pulled down they were all mixed together: pictures of musicians I'd cut out from magazines as a teenager, their corners oily with Blu-Tack from years stuck to my bedroom wall; lines of poetry that I'd written out in shiny black ink on scraps of paper; found photographs of strangers. There was ephemera relating to a moon-themed birthday party, including the shopping list of party supplies, the invitation, and a photocopied illustration of lunar animals that was produced as part of the Great Moon Hoax of 1835, when the New York newspaper *The Sun* published a series of articles about the discovery of life on the moon. The lunar animals were women with bat wings, shown swooping over a river beside which unicorns grazed, and giant flamingos waded. Seeing this now I desired to join them on the cratered surface of this moon, where surely my transformation would not seem so abnormal.

There was a postcard of an amusement park with a rollercoaster and a castle built into seaside cliffs, the packaging from a Canadian brand of chewing gum called 'Thrills', a note written on a beer coaster from the Oxford Hotel, a photocopy of an elaborate beehive hairdo from a 1960s guide to home hair-styling, a polaroid photograph of a man in a red terry-towelling hat and blue shirt and shorts holding up a metre-long fish, a little paper card with the words 'you mean the world to me' written inside, and a postcard reproduction of a photo of Frida Kahlo holding two doves. There were birthday cards, scraps of facts cut out of magazines, and a copy of an advertisement I'd once posted on noticeboards when I was looking for a housemate, warning the prospective respondent that the house was 'full of books'.

I'd kept these scraps as if they were keys, able to unlock details I would otherwise be unable to call to mind. Each scrap fitted in with its echo in my memory like a puzzle piece as I remembered the times in which I had found them significant. The next sheaf that I pincered down from my back had on top of it a postcard from the Parisian taxidermy shop Deyrolle. The image was of a room lined with cabinets, around which are arranged snarling polar bears, lions and tigers, an albino ostrich, and lambs curled up around a black bear.

The store had smelled of wood and chemicals and the animals seemed on pause, as if they would at any second blink, or twitch or yawn. I remembered the front window display had been of two goats wearing business shirts. Then inside the store I stood beside a zebra, thinking how this was the closest I would ever be to one. In a nearby cabinet were three moles, arranged as if conspiring. The baby chickens on the top shelf cost 480 euro each. These images were clear in my memory, but the store itself and much of its collection had been destroyed by fire a year after I visited, and the shop was later rebuilt and restocked with different taxidermy animals.

It was hard work removing these objects from my back, and my joints ached from the effort of it. It required mental labour too: each scrap I took down was a memory, and I careened between places and times. Deyrolle, Paris, in 2007. Then 1999, in the narrow top-floor apartment just off Parramatta Road, typing out a quote from Patrick White's *Riders in the Chariot* on the computer that accrued so much dust inside it that one day, with a bang and a flare of flame, it expired. In 1984, standing assembled for a school photograph, the class wearing red shirts and green jumpers as if we were Christmas elves, led by Mrs Bright, who was the stern opposite of her name.

Some of the scraps were other peoples' memories, black-and-white snapshots I'd bought from antique stores or found in the pages of second-hand books. They featured conventional scenes and poses, people assembled for picnics or standing in their gardens with the family dog. These I had incorporated into my own memories, to illustrate my family's stories for which no photographs existed. Here was a photograph of a cat standing up on its back legs, stretching towards a biscuit being held out by a hand that protrudes from a black jacket-cuff at the corner of the frame. I had decided that this cat could be Binky Boodles, the cat that had belonged to my grandfather's uncle. My grandfather had sometimes told me stories about this cat which, even after sixty years, he remembered well. Like the gloomy Mrs Bright, its endearing name had honed its cruellest faculties, and it was notorious for its savage temperament and habit of jumping down from its gatepost perch onto startled passers-by.

Sunlight angled into the room, illuminating the dusty air, indicating that it was now late afternoon. The effort of transferring the ephemera from my back to the floor had taken me many hours, and now it lay strewn around me like confetti. Without the insulation of the mass of papers sunlight fell directly on my skin, which was thin and readily saturated by the heat. In the mirror I was now able to see that I had a shape something like a silverfish, with a pale, segmented body that had two brown stripes running from head to tail. I drew back from the glass. This unlikely form was me. In this state I could no longer tell where my memory truly resided. Was it in these papers, or in this body that recoiled from itself when it saw its reflection?

An urge came for me to move away from the light, and I scuttled up the wall to the ceiling, as easily as I had walked across the floor in my human form. I'd spent many hours staring at this ceiling. Sometimes in dreams I floated up towards it to view myself sleeping below, but I had never experienced this sensation bodily. My weight inverted and my feet gripped the wall. From this position the room looked chaotic, as if it had been searched through then abandoned in a hurry, leaving piles of papers and books and a rumpled bed in the centre.

As I rested there in the corner of the room, the scene below no longer seemed so directly connected to me. The papers lay like dry leaves, their energies spent. I curled into a circle and with the spinneret in my tail produced a fine silver thread with which I wove a covering, lacy as a shawl. I anchored it to the wall, and spun threads until they surrounded me in a thick cocoon. Inside it I readied myself for sleep, and my next transformation.

Gentle and Fierce

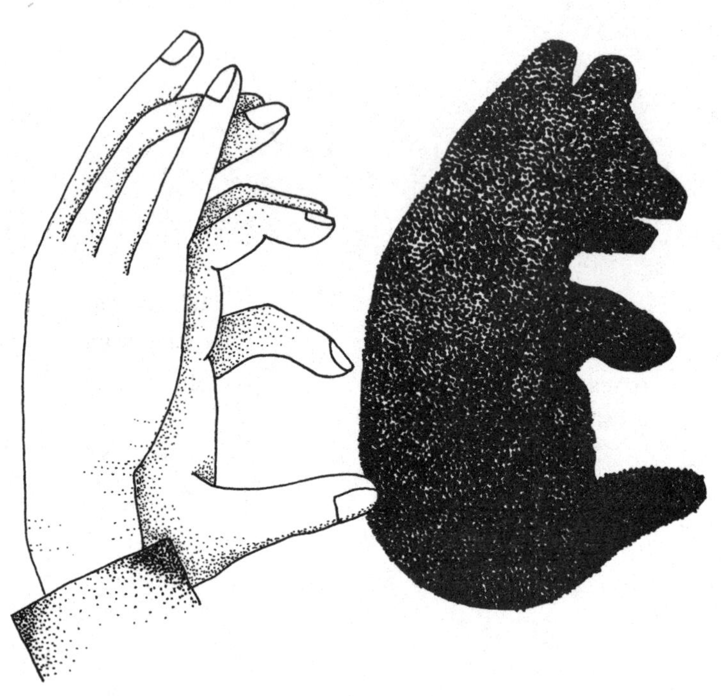

Gentle and Fierce

At the birthday party the children sat in a circle on the beige carpet of the living room, awaiting the next game. The two girls I was sitting between were, like me, wearing dresses with frills at the neck and cuffs. We wriggled, restless from the itch of our lacy collars. Attached to the wall behind us was a plastic banner which announced 'Happy Birthday' in rainbow lettering. The birthday girl was at the head of the circle, wearing a striped brown dress with a white trim. She looked like a Jersey Caramel, I thought, with sour intent. She and I were born on the same day, a fact which gave us a mild resentment of each other, each of us wishing the birthday was ours alone.

Her mother announced the game was to be animal charades. She passed around cards, each printed with a cartoon animal, cautioning us to keep our card a secret. I was a rabbit, I noted, before hiding my card under the hem of my dress. Her mother continued the instructions. We'll go around the circle, she said, and each person will choose someone to guess the identity of their animal. To help them guess, you must act out a charade.

The game began. A girl's swaying arm became an elephant's trunk, someone else scratched their armpits to become a monkey, another stood on one leg to become a flamingo. I dutifully brought my hands to my head to mime long ears, pursed my lips together in a pinched, long-toothed expression, and bounced up and down in a hop. Thankfully my performance was swiftly decoded by the girl I'd chosen as my partner.

Soon it was my turn to guess. The birthday girl in her caramel dress pointed at me, then puffed her arms out like a strongman and filled her cheeks with air. A cow, I said, and she shook her head, puffing her cheeks further, with such effort that I could see the veins bulging in her forehead. A puffer fish, I tried, but she continued to sway from side to side, with full cheeks and protruding arms. A pig, I said, although someone had already been a pig by pushing the tip of their nose up into a snout. She shook her head, keeping her cheeks inflated to bursting point.

The moment stretched out long and awkward. I might never be able to guess. She might never be able to breathe out. Her mother intervened, going into her own version of the puffy-faced, broad-armed gesture. She made noises, too, a low, groaning sound like a sick trombone as she loomed, red-faced, behind the circle of children. The animal that they were miming was a frightening thing, something ferocious. I searched my mind again, but had no answer. 'I don't know,' I said quietly, hoping a resolution would soon come.

Eventually, taking pity on me, the mother reached down to turn the card in her daughter's hand, revealing the cartoon face of a hippopotamus. 'A hippo!' she said, with one final puff of her cheeks. Her daughter looked smug at my failure but I felt only relief that my turn was over.

The party must have continued on, through games and cake, but my memory of it ends here. The thick beige loungeroom curtains draw across like theatre drapes, but the scene's peculiar combination of tensions linger on. It was one of the first moments in my life in which I experienced the power of choice. In the face of the bizarre mime that demanded my attention, I realised I didn't have to fight to resolve it. It was up to me to decide how to react. Which kind of animal would I be?

'You're a cat,' the man said, sidling up to me. The curtains open again and it is fifteen years later. Rather than the heavy brown drapes of a suburban house, the curtains are black velvet, and draw back to reveal a room in which a band is setting up on a makeshift stage.

It was the garage of an inner-city house that had been fitted out as a dungeon. Straps hung down from the ceiling and there were metal rings bolted into the walls, which were painted gloss-black. I'd come with some friends who were newly in love, and after pouring a measure of whisky into my plastic cup they turned to each other in intense conversation, their faces very close. I retreated to a high, padded bench on the opposite side of the room where I could sit alone and watch the band.

'A cat,' I repeated, imagining myself, in my white shirt and black trousers, as a black cat with a white chest. This outfit was unusual for me, as I mostly wore dresses, brightly coloured 1970s ones that were then plentiful in second-hand stores, but on this night I had dressed thinking myself like David Bowie, mid-1970s, reverting to black-and-white. A new disguise.

The man had a long, narrow face and slicked-back hair, and was wearing a brown, pin-striped suit, as if he'd walked out of a pulp fiction. 'What's your name, cat?' he asked.

'Petronella,' I said. I'd just read the Jean Rhys short story 'Till September Petronella', in which the main character drifts through scenes in which men treat her cruelly, and life is a series of disappointments and fleeting intimacies. It was the kind of wan, sad story that echoed my own indirection.

He looked as if he didn't believe me and went to say something more, but then a rush of sound filled the room as the band started up. The drummer hunched over the one snare drum and two cymbals that formed the kit, battering out a rhythm that seemed to quicken with every beat. As the beat raced a guitar swept in, and the singer reached for the microphone, her voice calm over the angry music, and everything was blanked out by the sound.

After the band finished, when the man asked for my phone number, I wrote down a fictional one to go with my fictional name. The friends I had come with were nowhere to be seen and so I slunk out the door, into the laneway. In the distance the darkness revealed a black cat. Its eyes flashed as it stared at me, before it lowered its body to the ground and disappeared so smoothly and quickly under a fence it was as if it had been inhaled by something on the other side.

I started on the walk home, swaying from the whisky, picking flowers from the well-tended gardens of the renovated houses. I lived in the other kind, a house long overdue for refurbishment or demolition. It hadn't been updated in my lifetime at least. In the bathroom was an old gas water heater which, when I turned on the tap, came to life with a whoosh of blue flames inside. On the metal casing was the face of a rabbit with long ears and a lean face, a malevolent magician's assistant. It waited for my return.

The night grows deeper, darker, it swallows the rest of the memory. When light returns to the sky Petronella is gone. She left with the black cat in the laneway, disappeared with the whoosh of the hot water rabbit. I long ago stepped out of her costume.

The light comes in weakly, through two long, thin windows, and stumbles over the room's clutter. The desk is piled with papers, and beside it is an overladen clothes rack, sagging under the weight of the dresses squeezed onto it. The mantelpiece is decorated by figures of animals, a domestic natural history display of plastic and paper specimens. They form an irregular parade: a rubber elephant with wrinkled pink skin like a weird baby, a dodo made of *papier mâché* and feathers, a flat cardboard pig on a stand, its long thin legs rising from a base of synthetic fluff.

The image of the flat pigs had come to me in a dream, in which I was in a muddy wasteland, my feet stuck fast as I watched pigs in a neighbouring yard. They were flat like fleas and ran on long, spindly legs through a pale cloud-like substance. As odd as they were I regarded them tenderly. While I was weighed down in the heavy silt, the pigs were light and free amid their habitat of clouds.

My dreams were often of things obscured, unlit city streets or a fishbowl full of orange juice in which goldfish circled. These murky scenes reflected the indecision of my waking life. I was in love with two people and my head and my heart were divided. The thought of forgoing either path made me so heavy I could not move in any direction. As hard as I tried to think my way through it, I couldn't. This time no one was going to take pity on me and reveal the card with the answer.

After I told Simon the dream of the flat pigs, and how despite their strangeness I'd found them consoling, he had set about making a herd of them from cardboard and wire. A few days afterwards, hearing scuffling outside, I opened the front door to find them arranged on the steps. Compared to my room where I lay in bed with my stuck thoughts, the pigs on the steps were light creatures with their feet in the clouds. I took them inside and added one to the procession of animals across the mantelpiece.

As the day continued the sunlight moved across the ceiling,

forming patterns and extending shadows. The animals grew new, different silhouettes. On the wall behind it the dodo became a cloaked figure with a long nose, like a storybook witch. The elephant turned into a waving ghost. The flat pig now had the wide body of a stingray. When I stood up my own shadow stretched across the wall. It too was something else, a bear, wide and hunched, close behind me, copying my movements.

I turned around, trying to catch my shadow out, but the bear was too quick and had already followed me to face in the other direction. The further away from it I moved the larger it grew, swelling to fill the wall and then the room, obscuring the rest of the night. But under the cover of its shadow a decision was taking shape. Soon afterwards I stepped off the wheel of hesitancy that I had been following round and round.

'You're a camel, you know, a camel,' the palm reader said, as she grasped my hand firmly on her lap, jabbing at the lines on my hand with a blue biro. We sat on milk crates against the yellow-tiled wall of the pedestrian tunnel underneath Central station, as commuters charged past. Behind her was a handwritten sign on a square of cardboard advertising her services as a 'Palm Reader and Face Reader'. Most days she could be found set up here at the end of the tunnel, staunchly waiting, eyes magnified behind thick bifocal glasses as crowds rushed by.

Her voice was high and relentless, like a preacher speaking of salvation, as she explained my camel nature. You should not live near water, she said, and if you live in the mountains, no fire will burn you. You are safe with heights, safe with tall buildings, you will not die in a plane crash. She took the blue biro to my palm, the fleshy part below my thumb, to write a sequence of numbers. One o'clock, she said, is your best time of day, the time you should get married, or divorced. Seventy-two, if you don't do yoga every fortnight, you will be shrivelled and sick by this age. Ninety-two, this is how many years you will live.

Camel, she repeated. You can move north, south, east, west. Eat red apples, buy red flowers. These are not for you, she said, pointing to the bunch of bluebells that were poked into the side pocket of my bag. She leaned in close to my face to scrutinise it, and then sat back. This is not your year, she said, I'm sorry. But you are lucky. You are sensible. Do not listen to other people.

I gave her the twenty dollars that was her fee and walked the rest of the tunnel with my head a whirl of predictions. She was right, at least, that it had not been my year. Year of inertia, year of the forking paths, but now that I had chosen my way I was resilient, able to travel great distances, drawing on my inner resources. When I emerged from the tunnel, out into the street, I saw the face of the station clock, high up in the tower. The minute hand rested a few notches away from one, the time she had promised was mine.

The plastic wall clock clicked through the seconds, counting the time in a country town hair salon. For the annual contemporary art festival the salon had been repurposed as an artist's studio. The front window was decorated with drawings of spirals and caterpillars, behind which a chair had been set up. A woman was sitting in it, and a man wearing a loose grey sweater was standing behind her, holding up a sheet of tracing paper to the back of her head. Working quickly, he copied the shape of her head onto the page, the line following her silhouette. 'He reads the crowns of people's heads,' an assistant standing in the doorway told us. 'Then after tracing them he draws the animals he sees as residing there.'

We waited our turn on the couch at the side of the room, watching the woman's crown-animal take shape. It became an orange insect, with six bright, short legs, and she laughed when she saw it, happy or surprised. Then it was Simon's turn. He took up his position in the chair and the artist held a sheet of translucent paper up to the crown of his head to trace it. Then the artist used a blue pen to draw a long, curled loop at the top, the tongue for an animal that took the shape of an echidna, with flicks of brown ink for spines.

When it was my turn I sat in the chair and listened to the sound of the paper by my ears, thinking about the crown of my head and what energy it might emit. I perceived my body as a shape, an outline, with the elusive thing that is my spirit contained within it, hiding or emerging as the pen moved over the paper.

Having drawn the outline the artist moved down to the floor and leaned low over the drawing, adding a triangular shape onto the top. My outline became a long body striped with blue streaks. He added four flippers and a tail, and two jagged scribbles as rows of sharp teeth on either side of its triangular head. At the top of the page he drew two smaller versions of the main figure, again with flippers and zigzag teeth. This was my portrait. It hadn't been what I expected.

'Crocodiles,' he said. 'A mother crocodile and baby crocodiles.' I held the drawing up to examine it, decoding what had been transmitted. I was three figures in one, the smaller two protected by the larger, all with the same sharp teeth and long tails, an image gentle and fierce.

Notes

Jonathan Swift's *Cadenus and Vanessa* was first published in 1726, as was *Gulliver's Travels.*

The issue of the *National Geographic* with the story of the monarch's overwintering place is Vol. 150, No. 2, August 1976.

Cat Catalog: the ultimate cat book edited by Judy Fireman, was published by Sun Books, Melbourne, in 1977.

Life in a Rotten Log by Kathie Atkinson was published by Allen and Unwin in 1993.

'Twittering machine' is a reference to the artwork *Die Zwitscher-Maschine* by Paul Klee (1922).

Emily Dickinson's 'I heard a fly buzz – when I died –' was written in 1862 and first published in 1896.

'A force in things which one had overlooked', quoted in 'The Fly', is from Virginia Woolf's *A Room of One's Own,* first published in 1929 by Hogarth Press.

Michael Ende's novel *The Neverending Story* was published in English translation by Ralph Manheim in 1983, and the film version, directed by Wolfgang Petersen, was released in 1984.

The Secret Language of Birthdays is by Gary Goldschneider and was first published in 1994 by Penguin.

'Lady Lazarus' and 'The Couriers' by Sylvia Plath are from *Ariel,* published in 1965 by Faber and Faber. Plath's *The Bell Jar* was first published in 1963 by Heinemann.

Walter Benjamin's *Berlin Childhood Around 1900* was first published in 1950, and in English translation, by Howard Eiland, in 2006 by the Belknap Press.

The song 'Lullaby' is from the 1989 album by The Cure, *Disintegration*. The video is directed by Tim Pope.

Georges Perec's *Life: A User's Manual* was first published in 1978, and in English translation by David Bellos in 1987. Perec's *An Attempt at Exhausting a Place in Paris* was first published in 1975 and published in English translation by Marc Lowenthal in 2010. His 1976 essay 'Notes on the Objects to Be Found on My Desk' was published in *Thoughts of Sorts*, translated by David Bellos, in 2009, by Verba Mundi.

The Old Irish poem 'Pangur Bán' is found in the Reichenau Primer, and was written in the ninth century by an unknown Irish monk.

Natsume Soseki's *I Am a Cat* was first published in 1906 and then in 1972 in English translation by Graeme Wilson by Tuttle Publishing.

'Lassie and the Eagle' was first broadcast in 1962, and directed by William Beaudine.

Lassie Come-Home by Eric Knight was first published in 1940 by the John C. Winston Company.

World of Strange Animals by V.J. Staněk was published in its English translation by Joe Kadečková, by Paul Hamlyn in 1966.

The description 'fire should move like water' was from Jason De Santolo, reading for the *Sydney Review of Books* in 2019, at Frontyard, Gadigal country, Marrickville.

'Ancestral stories of dawn and fire' refers to the Wathaurong story 'Maeewan nyanbo meerree' as re-told by Uncle David Tournier, and the Adnyamathanha story told in *The Magpie and the Crow* by Terrence Coulthard, Cliff Coulthard and Buck

McKenzie, published by Harcourt Brace Jovanovich in 1987.

The crown portraits described in the essay 'Gentle and Fierce' were drawn by the artist Thom Roberts.

Acknowledgements

I live and work on Gadigal land, and it is here that much of *Gentle and Fierce* was written. I offer my gratitude and respect to Gadigal people and acknowledge their ongoing care of country. My acknowledgement and gratitude also goes to the Yuin and Worimi peoples on whose lands I spent short but significant periods of time working on this book. I respectfully acknowledge Aboriginal kinship relationships, the wisdom and knowledge embedded within these systems, and the enduring interconnections between Aboriginal people and land, water, animals, plants, cycles and stories.

To my friends, family, mentors, teachers, colleagues, correspondents, students, and followers, I offer my thanks; I carry your support and influence with me. To the zine, literary and visual arts communities that I am fortunate to be a part of, thank you for nurturing and sustaining me. For bringing this book into being, and their support of my creative work, thank you to Giramondo, and to Jane Novak.

For the writing of *Gentle and Fierce* I received project funding from the Australia Council for the Arts, and offer my thanks for this assistance. Residencies at Bundanon Trust and the Gunyah Artist Residency provided time and space to allow these essays to take shape, my gratitude to both residency programs for this important support.

About the author

Vanessa Berry is a writer who works with memory, history, archives and objects. She is the author of *Mirror Sydney: An Atlas of Reflections*, an essay collection on the urban environment; the memoirs *Ninety9* and *Strawberry Hills Forever*; and the autobiographical zine series *I Am a Camera*. Her zine and illustration works have been exhibited at major Australian galleries including the Museum of Contemporary Art and National Gallery of Australia. She is a Lecturer in Creative Writing at the University of Sydney.